99 Things to Save Money in Your Household Budget

99 Things to Save Money in Your Household Budget

Mary Hance
a.k.a. Ms.Cheap

TRADE PAPER
PRESS

Those who have little, if they are good at managing, must be accounted among the rich.

~Socrates

Turner Publishing Company
200 4th Avenue North • Suite 950
Nashville, Tennessee 37219
(615) 255-2665

www.turnerpublishing.com

99 Things to Save Money in Your Household Budget

Library of Congress Cataloging-in-Publication Data

Hance, Mary, 1953-
99 things to save money in your household budget / by Mary Hance.
    p. cm.
Includes bibliographical references.
ISBN 978-1-59652-547-4
1. Home economics--Accounting. 2. Budgets, Personal. 3. Consumer education. I. Title. II. Title: Ninety nine things to save money in your household budget.
TX326.H25 2009
332.024--dc22

2009016359

Printed in China

09 10 11 12 13 14 15 16—0 9 8 7 6 5 4 3 2

Economy is the art of making the most of life.

~George Bernard Shaw

Contents

Introduction

If there ever was a time to find creative ways to do more with less, that time is right now.

Everybody I know wants—and needs—more money. Common logic tells us that the most effective and realistic way to meet that goal is to spend less money.

I know it's not as simple as declaring a moratorium on shopping or freezing your credit card in a block of ice. But it can be done.

Saving money is definitely more fun when it is not essential, but either way, doing more with less requires a new way of thinking and prioritizing—and it needs to be done in a way that is in sync with your values.

I like to look at it as stewardship—being a good steward of your money.

The question is not whether to be cheap or not to be cheap. Rather, the question is whether you want to manage your money in such a way that you sacrifice on some things in order to spend on other things you deem to be more important.

It is mostly a matter of prioritizing, thinking about your purchases, and being creative with your spending. It will also require some serious changes in your mindset, as well as a steady dose of self-discipline. But the result—of living comfortably within your means—is so worth it.

The "doing more with less" mentality is easier said than done, so what I am offering you in this little book are tips and tactics to help you creatively stretch your hard-earned dollars. These 99 things will simplify your life, allowing you to be who you are and do what you enjoy without going beyond your means.

Here are some things to think about:

Happiness is not having what you want,
but wanting what you have.
~Rabbi H. Schachtel

Because of taxes, a penny saved is worth more than a penny earned.

Only people who like dog food don't save for retirement.
~Dave Ramsey,
author of *Financial Peace*

Spending less is better than earning more.
~Paul A. Wilson, author of
Real Men Use Coupons

In my opinion, "cheapskate" *now describes a very classy and dignified individual who saves consistently and spends less than he or she earns.*
~Mary Hunt, editor of *Debt-Proof Living*
and *Everyday Cheapskate*

Without frugality none can be rich, and with it very few would be poor.
~Samuel Johnson

Never spend your money before you have earned it.
~Thomas Jefferson

Beware of little expenses; a small leak will sink a great ship.
~Benjamin Franklin

My grandfather's motto is still the best advice I've heard: "One way to make money is not to spend it."
~Michael Eisner, former Disney CEO

There must be more to life than having everything.
~Maurice Sendak,
best-selling children's author

Nothing is cheap which is superfluous, for what one does not need is dear at a penny.
~Plutarch

The key is to keep short-term wants from taking priority over long-term needs.
~Ginger Applegarth from *The Money Diet*

Don't tell me where your priorities are. Show me where you spend your money and I'll tell you what they are.
~James W. Frick, author

One of the best ways to measure people is to watch the way they behave when something free is offered.
~Ann Landers

Money will not make you happy, and happy will not make you money.
~Groucho Marx

You should never skimp on brakes or parachutes.
~*Savvy Discounts* newsletter

They that go a-borrowing, go a-sorrowing.
~John Clarke

Money makes money, and the money that money makes, makes more money.
~Benjamin Franklin

Ere you consult your fancy, consult your purse.
~Benjamin Franklin

The 99 Things

– 1 –

Have a budget

I know that creating a budget is not a fun exercise, but it is something that everyone can and should do to gain control of their financial life. People say they don't want to be restricted by a budget, but the truth is that a budget is in many ways very freeing. If you don't save for a vacation, chances are you won't have the money to take that vacation when the time comes. If you don't save for a down payment on a house, it will be hard to come up with it when the time is right to buy.

I'm certainly not an investment advisor, but I know that if we don't have a plan, we are headed for trouble. And I know that if we don't deliberately save money, it is not magically going to appear in our bank accounts.

It is so important to get a grip on your current situation. You need to know where all of your money is coming from and where it is all going before you can make any effective changes.

- Do you know your net worth?
- Do you know how much money you really spend each month?
- Do you save any money from each paycheck for a cushion?

These are good questions to ask yourself.

The first step to creating a budget is to write down what you take in every month and what you spend every month. Take your time on this and be sure to think of *everything* you spend—including the cup of coffee on the way to work, the occasional lunch out, the gifts for special birthdays or holidays, the cost of entertaining, your gifts to charity or your church, insurance, taxes, and all of those little incidentals that don't seem like much but often add up to more than you think.

I read recently that 48 percent of Americans suffer from "mystery spending." The study revealed that we "lose track" on average of $2,340 annually. Americans say they can't account for more than a third of their cash—spending an average of $120 a week but losing track of $45.

Then look at your total after-tax income—and compare the two to see where you come out.

One of my newspaper readers, Ed King, sent me this quip: "If your outgo is more than your income, then your upkeep will be your downfall."

– 2 –
Just say no

In challenging times, we have to say *no* to things that are just plain frivolous. Saying no is hard because we are so accustomed to saying yes. The advertisers and marketers have pretty much brainwashed us into thinking we need to say yes to makeup and plastic surgery and sexual aids and toys and hair color, and handbags and cruises and extravagant weddings, and bigger houses and swimming pools and sexy shoes, and luxurious sheets and on and on and on.

The truth is that we have to be strong and say no to a lot of things—so that we will have the money for the things we truly want and need to make our lives richer.

— 3 —

Face the reality of your buying habits

Financial planner Stacy Johnson of *Money Talks* told me when he was in Nashville about an exercise that he has all his financial planning clients do before they really get down to business. He has them walk around their home and write down everything they bought that they don't need, don't use, don't wear.

Then he instructs them to write down, to the best of their recollection, what they paid for each thing and then add it up. Obviously the goal is to help people see that buying this little gadget and that little knickknack and this belt and that purse—none of which does anything to really improve the quality of life—adds up to big bucks. And then he challenges them to think what could be done with that money—for themselves or someone else—if they had *not* bought all of those "little things."

– 4 –

Ask, ask, ask

If you don't ask, you don't get. It really is that simple. If you see something you want, ask the clerk if they can do better on the price, ask if they know when it might go on sale, ask if you can call back in a few days to see if the price has dropped.

If the item has any kind of blemish, ask if the store can give you a little break on the price. If the business is a local independent, ask if you can pay cash and get a discount, since they won't have to pay the credit card company.

The bottom line is that it never hurts to ask. The worst that can happen is that they will say no.

And the "asking" strategy is not just for retail.

I recently heard a story about someone who miscalculated a bank deposit and had a check bounce.

Of course the bank charged her an arm and a leg, and that caused a second check to bounce and the bank charged her another arm and leg.

As soon as she realized her mistake, she hightailed it over to the bank and spoke with the manager and politely asked if the charges could be waived since her record was otherwise perfect. Done deal! The manager took care of it.

The moral is that when you detect a problem, don't just pay whatever it is and let it go. If you have a good record and are willing to plead your case, go for it. The best bet is to gain access to a manager or other person who can actually do something about it.

Another story I heard was from a woman who called a magazine she subscribed to and told them that she couldn't afford a subscription at the full price. Well, lo and behold, they gave her a discount.

A young mother told me that when her daughter was born, they owed $800 to the hospital after insurance. "I called the billing department and said I wanted to pay in full if they could give me a discount. They knocked 20 percent off, saving us $160."

You need to stick up for yourself when things are not right. A few weeks ago, I ordered 50 pieces of fried chicken at my neighborhood grocery to take to a program for the homeless that our church sponsors. When I got to church and started transferring the chicken to a platter for serving, I didn't think it looked like 50 pieces of chicken, and so I started counting. Sure enough, it was only 44 pieces of chicken. A lot of people would have just let it go, but I believe we are obligated to make sure we are treated fairly and honestly. I called the store manager the following morning and told him what had happened and let him know that I was really ticked off about it. He instantly offered me a super special on the chicken the next time I am one of the hosts of the feeding program. Believe me, I will take him up on it.

And one of the most overlooked discounts that involves being proactive is the senior discount, which kicks in anywhere from age 50 to 65. The problem is that most businesses will *not* ask if you are a senior—you must do the asking. I think you'll be surprised at how many businesses have the discounts but don't advertise them.

— 5 —

Make yourself save
something every month

It seems that Americans have pretty much stopped saving for a rainy day and gone with the living-paycheck-to-paycheck way of life. The problem is that there's always plenty of precipitation in the forecast.

According to Stephen Brobeck, executive director of Consumer Federation of America, too many Americans don't understand their financial condition and don't have realistic savings—or spending—plans.

The easiest way to get in the savings habit is to have something taken out of every paycheck before you ever see it. I talked to some really savvy savers who say that when they get a raise, they have a portion of the new money taken out for savings since they are not used to having it anyway. My husband saves all the change from his pockets every night and puts it in a huge piggy bank. Then we periodically raid it when there is an emergency expenditure or when it is time to go on vacation or there is some other extra that we want or need. A Christmas Club savings account is another good idea. The point is to make yourself save something—even when times are tough. It really does add up faster than you think, especially if you can start young and be consistent—not only because it enables you to take advantage of the compound interest for earnings purposes, but also because the savings habit is something you can build on as your situation improves.

Even if you save $1 a day . . .

– 6 –

Quiz yourself before you buy anything

This list of questions comes from the University of Tennessee Extension Service, and I like to keep it in my purse as a reminder to myself from time to time. Before you buy anything, ask yourself:

- Do I really need it?
- Do I have something that will be a good substitute for it?
- Can I postpone the purchase?
- Does anybody I know have one I can borrow?
- Do I already have one?
- Can I shop around and get a better deal?

This sounds so basic, but asking yourself these questions and answering them honestly can definitely keep you from buying on impulse. The goal is to talk yourself out of buying unnecessary things.

One reader told me that she puts her credit card in a block of ice so that she cannot make impulse purchases. Another says she leaves her cash and cards at home when she shops—forcing her to make a special return trip if she decides to make a purchase.

In her column "Everyday Cheapskate," guru Mary Hunt has some other questions and tactics to help us ward off our compulsive buying tendencies:

"Parent yourself: When tempted to give in to my demands to have what I want and have it right now, I ask myself, 'Would I accept from my children the type of behavior that I'm about to accept from myself?' Seeing my behavior as that of a spoiled bratty kid usually stops me dead in my tracks.

"Avoid 'slippery' places: Alcoholics Anonymous defines a slippery place as any situation that will provide a tempting opportunity to drink. My slippery places are stores, television shopping channels, slick advertisements and mail order catalogs. If I don't frequent them, I'm not tempted.

"Make spending difficult: Think of all the ways our culture makes spending money so convenient: checkbooks, credit cards, debit cards, deferred payment, equity lines of credit, electronic transfers, and on it goes. I choose to take the convenience out of spending. I carry enough cash to meet my needs for the day. Sometimes it's a pain, but I do avoid many opportunities to act compulsively.

"Talk to yourself: When confronted with a tempting purchase, self-talk is my lifesaver: 'If this weren't on sale would you still buy it?' If the answer is no, I pass," Hunt says.

― 7 ―
Carry a "buy-at-the-right-price" list

This is a list of things you would like to have but don't need immediately (or maybe at all).

The idea is to have all the details at hand, such as measurements or other particulars, so that if you run across the item at a yard sale, thrift store, or online, you can be sure that it meets your need.

For example, if you'd like to have a set of miniblinds for the guest room, or a rug for the den, write down the measurements and do a little research to determine what the retail price is so that you'll know a true bargain. You surely don't want to buy things that you can't even use because they don't fit.

~ 8 ~

Keep in mind that nothing is a bargain unless you need it

This one is a challenge for me because my job as a frugal consumer columnist requires me to be at stores and sales all the time—and I almost always see some kind of tempting deal. I hear stories all the time from bargain hunters who tell me about "too good to pass up" deals. I wrote in my newspaper column about a little shoe store that a local shoe designer had set up temporarily to sell his shoes at 70 percent below the suggested retail. One of my readers called to thank me for letting her know about the deals at the shop and excitedly reported that she had bought ten pair of shoes on her first visit to the store and was considering a return trip. Now, who, pray tell, *needs* another *ten* pair of shoes? I have to keep telling myself, nothing is a bargain unless you need it, nothing is a bargain unless you need it, nothing is a bargain. . . .

The trick is to focus on what you really need. If you can make the distinction between need and want and stick with the needs and let go of the wants, you have more than half the battle won.

It seems to me that so much of what gets us into financial trouble is impulse purchasing—and slipping into the all-too-easy habit of buying things we see that we like without really thinking the purchases all the way through. Instant gratification is not always (or not even usually) a good thing.

Keeping this focus definitely requires discipline and self-examination, but it really is the only way to keep ourselves on the leaner paths we are setting for ourselves.

If you say *no* to the "wants" and try to get the best price on the needs, you are on the right road.

– 9 –

Evaluate your insurance policies at least annually

I read recently that one in four people mistakenly believes that all car insurance companies charge the same rates. Shopping around can pay off—and even if you don't find something better, you have the peace of mind of knowing you are getting the best price.

It's wise to contact your agent at least annually to see if the rate has possibly changed or if there are new options. You might find that raising a deductible or making other adjustments can save you some serious money.

Look for every discount possible—being a good student, having multiple policies bundled with one insurer, taking driver education or senior driver classes. Having good credit can also have a bearing on your rates.

On the home front, with houses decreasing in value these days, make sure you don't have too much insurance, and be sure that you are just insuring the house itself and not the land it sits on.

And make this evaluation an annual exercise—just routinely rolling over policies from year to year without reevaluating can mean missing out on some savings. Also, think twice before filing small claims—it may not be worth it to file if the damage is about the same as the deductible.

$-$ 10 $-$

Pay your credit card bill in full every single month

Some credit card companies charge over 20 percent in interest and you are getting absolutely nothing for it. Late fees can kill you, too. If you see that you can't pay in full and on time, you may need to cut up your credit card and become a cash-only person.

The real deal is having a credit card that is working for you—as in paying you to use it. Cards like Discover, some of the gas company or airline cards, or the Capital One rewards card pays returns based on your usage. To me that is convenience, as well as free money for you.

Check www.cardratings.com for comparisons of the various cards and their perks and rates.

– 11 –

Think long and hard before getting a pet

I am not saying absolutely to *not* get a dog or cat (we have a wonderful German shepherd named Shoogar), but I am saying to go into pet ownership with your eyes wide open. The annual expense for a large dog can top $2,000 when you consider food, equipment, licenses, training, occasional boarding, and of course the inevitable vet bills. If you do decide to go ahead with a pet, consider adopting one from the shelter instead of buying a purebred. And by all means, shop around for a vet. You'd be surprised at how much the fees vary. A good way to do it would be to call around to several clinics and ask for prices for basic procedures like neutering and for rabies vaccinations. That should give you a good idea of what their pricing structure is. Another savings tactic is

21

instead of paying to board your pet when you have to be away, try to set up a pet-sitting exchange with other pet owner pals and help each other out.

One more thing—don't think that if you have to have a pet that it must be a cat or dog. How about a fish or maybe a hermit crab? They may not be as cuddly, but they won't rumple your budget either. Just an idea!

– 12 –
Think cheap fitness

You don't have to have a gym membership to work out. There are so many cheap and free options, starting with workout videos you can buy or check out from the library. A set of hand weights can be purchased for under $10, and the Internet is a great source for identifying exercises for your routine. You can literally turn your living room or bedroom into a fitness center with a yoga or exercise mat, a set of dumbbells, and maybe one of those exercise balls.

Even easier is just walking in your neighborhood or park. Check with your local park system to learn of any fitness classes and facilities they offer free-of-charge. In Nashville, for example, where I live, there are regional community centers with indoor pools, indoor tracks, gyms, and an array of fitness classes—

paid for with our tax dollars—so we may as well take advantage of them.

And if you just have to have something more formal, check with your Y.M.C.A. or other gym for any programs they offer where you can volunteer a certain number of hours a month to get a free or reduced-price membership.

— 13 —

Take your lunch
(at least two or three days a week)

This is such a no-brainer. Lunch out can get expensive—even at fast food and discount places. Let's say that you spend even $5 a day for lunch five days a week. That comes to about $1,000 a year just for lunches. And as you know, it's increasingly challenging to find a decent $5 lunch.

That thousand bucks could be money for a trip or a giant TV and an iPod or lots of other good things more lasting than a daily lunch out.

A good way to make the lunch preparation easy and super cheap (if you have access to a microwave at work) is to deliberately plan enough dinner to have lunch leftovers.

I've also heard of some families who have an assembly line for making the whole group's lunches in one fell swoop. It could even be fun!

And I've heard of lunch-bunch groups at work where one person will make enough soup or chili or sandwiches or another dish for the whole group one day a week, so the burden is shared. Sandwiches and soups are so easy, but a nice salad or pasta dish works well on the cheapometer, too.

Packing a lunch or a picnic cooler is also a wise move when traveling or going as a group on an all-day outing to a theme park or attraction like the zoo or museum, or when you go on a nature hike. I love a picnic and it can be so inexpensive.

– 14 –
Sleep on it

This is an expression I've heard most of my life from my frugal parents and grandparents, who all believed in taking their precious time before buying just about anything. They were right that postponing a purchase really can bring clarity.

Impulse buying is what drives retail, and if you can just walk away, go home, and think about it, many times you realize that you don't need or want whatever it is all that much after all.

Postponing works very well for me. If I want something, I tell myself that I won't buy it today, that I will come back later to get it. Chances are that I won't go back. It is more likely that I will get home and think, Oh, I don't need that, or even get home and find that I already have something remarkably similar that is just about as good as what I was getting ready to shell out my hard-earned money for.

Or I just get busy and don't make it back to the store. Either way, it helps to keep me from buying things that I didn't really need anyway.

And if you do decide that after all, you really must have whatever it is, "sleeping on it" may give you the chance to negotiate or to shop around and get a better deal.

~ 15 ~
Shop garage sales for bargains

Shopping garage sales for bargains is a wonderful way to get all sorts of things for pennies on the dollar. There is definitely the "thrill of the hunt" involved in this kind of shopping.

Here are some tips for shoppers:

- Be first to the sales. That way you get first pick.
- Know what you are looking for—have sizes and measurements with you if you are looking for furniture, rugs, or clothes.
- Hit the high-end neighborhoods first.
- The opposite advice is to shop late in the sale when the prices are most negotiable.
- Either way, never buy anything you can't use or don't have a plan for.

- At the same time, be open-minded—and look at items creatively.
- Take cash in small denominations and some change. It is easier to negotiate a lower price when the seller sees the cash.
- Take a tape measure and measure the item.
- Use the newspaper and craigslist.com to find sales, then prioritize them as to interest and what time they start.
- Negotiate. You should almost always offer less, but in some cases, if you think the price is firm or that someone else will scoop you, you can justify paying full price.
- If you want something but don't want to pay the asking price, make an offer and arrange to call later in the day to see if the price has been lowered.
- The more you go to the sales, the more you will learn about prices—what's fair and what's high.
- Buy what you like, but also buy quality.
- Have fun shopping.

– 16 –
Have a garage sale

There are two good reasons to have a yard sale: to get rid of stuff you no longer need or want and to make money. If you have stuff to unload and you price it right, your sale is bound to be a success. Honestly, I don't believe there is really any way to screw one up. Bad weather, road closings, other unfortunate circumstances—nothing seems to deter determined shoppers . . . if you have the goods.

Having a sale is hard work, but oh-so-satisfying at the end of the day.

Here are some strategies and tips that will make it easier for you to sell your castoffs and maximize your proceeds.

• Start your preparations in plenty of time to check

every closet, every corner of the garage, and under every bed looking for merchandise. You can't make money on things you don't put in the sale.

• Price things to sell based on what you think you might pay for the used item, not what you paid for it new. I think it is best to price everything individually. It is time-consuming, but shoppers don't like a mystery. They need a ballpark price to know where to start negotiating.

• Have a specific goal for the money you make. It's a good idea to get the whole family involved. If you have a common objective like a family trip or a new DVD player, it makes everybody more willing to relinquish items to the sale.

• Let shoppers know you're willing to bargain. When they arrive, tell them to make an offer if they see something they want.

• If your sale is to benefit a good cause, let shoppers know it. Oftentimes they will give you a little more if they know the money is going to something worthwhile.

• Make sure you have good, well-placed signs directing people to your sale, and put them up at least a day ahead or maybe more if you have a good, high-traffic area nearby. Write large enough for people traveling in a car to see the details. And be sure to take the signs down when your sale is over.

• Place an ad in the newspaper. I know this sounds self-serving since I am a newspaper reporter, but believe me, people do plan their shopping routes by the newspaper.

• Advertise with a flourish. Don't just say "yard sale." Be specific. If it is a moving sale or an estate sale, say so (though many shoppers I talked to get irritated when organizers use "estate sale" in ads when their sales were really plain old garage sales). "Priced to sell" is another attractive enticement.

• Also, if it is a five-family affair, say so, since that will be a bigger draw than a single-family sale. Being creative is good, too. One recent ad I saw said, "Early birds will be barbecued!" Good directions are also worth including.

• Have a "bid box" for big-ticket items. That way, if someone is interested in a certain item and makes a low offer, you can get them to write down their name and number for future reference. Then you can call them at the end of the day if you don't get a better offer—if, of course, you still want to get rid of whatever it is.

• Set up a table of free things that you just want out of your house. One year I put out a huge stack of gift boxes I had accumulated. Another year I put out an embarrassing bunch of those annoying wire coat hangers. Amazingly, both found some takers, and I didn't have the guilt or hassle of throwing them away.

• Have a plan for the sale's leftovers. My garage sale rule usually is: What comes out to the sale is not allowed back in the house. This keeps my getting-rid-of mission intact. Many charities will pick up your leftovers if you call ahead and make arrangements.

• Don't forget the basics, such as having enough change to make change through the day ($1 bills and quarters primarily), and safety tips, such as having a cell phone outside with you.

• Remember to keep your money safe, in a pocket

or pouch on your person, and don't let shoppers in your house.

• Last but not least, have fun!

If you want to have a neighborhood sale: Having a full-blown neighborhood yard sale has lots of advantages, such as the likelihood you'll attract more shoppers. Also, it makes your advertising costs cheaper, since everybody pitches in toward a newspaper ad and easier since you can share the work of putting up signs.

It's easy to put one together, and it definitely increases your chances for individual success.

Here are a few pointers for putting on a neighborhood sale.

• Put out fliers in the neighborhood three or four weeks before the designated day, alerting neighbors of the opportunity to join in and asking them to sign up with their address and $5 (or more or less, depending on the size of the neighborhood and the cost of the ad).

• Have a deadline for participants to get the money and address information back to you so that you can compile your newspaper ad. It might read something like: "Neighborhood sale, 31 families participating," followed by a list of all the sale addresses.

• Make arrangements for an organization to show up immediately after the sale to pick up everybody's leftovers. You should find plenty of takers, since the organization will get lots of salable merchandise instead of just a few from one house.

• Decide on a symbol, such as balloons or some other ornament, to help shoppers find individual sales.

• Celebrate with a party afterward.

– 17 –
Shop thrift stores

I warn you that this can be addictive because once you find a great bargain—say a Coach handbag for $4.99 or a piece of Waterford crystal for $1.98—you are hooked for life. I do love thrift stores because they offer such good deals and almost all benefit worthy programs and organizations at the same time.

The best tips for shopping thrift stores are:

• Stop by often because they are putting new things out all the time.

• Think outside the box. Most people think of thrift stores being the place to buy clothes, but there is a lot more. Say, the carafe of your Mr. Coffee was broken—these stores are the place to look because they seem to have every make and model for just a few bucks. I also hear from readers who buy clothes just for the buttons, and I often buy picture frames and remove the picture so that I can frame something special of my own.

• Go with an open mind because it really is like a treasure hunt.

• At the same time, have a list of things you are looking for along with sizes or measurements so that you can pounce if you find just what you are looking for.

• Inspect everything carefully for stains, zippers that don't work, and other blemishes before you check out.

One more thing—thrift stores have become much more sophisticated, so get to know their perks and programs so that you can get the most out of your shopping.

For example, our Goodwill stores in Middle Tennessee have storewide half-price days the first Saturday of every month. Our Salvation Army stores offer half price on clothes all day every Wednesday. Many of the stores have loyalty programs or clubs that give regular shoppers and donors extra deals. Many have senior discounts and calendars that list specials on certain days—half-price books on one day, all clothes 25 percent off another day, linens half off another.

I also like to know the missions of the various stores so that I can feel even better about what I spend.

– 18 –
Do it yourself

I mean *everything* that you can do yourself—whether it is gardening, yard work, painting, sewing, cleaning house, ironing, cooking, shopping, framing pictures, painting your own nails, washing your dog—do it yourself.

Some of my readers even say they cut and color their own hair. Not me. I just know if I cut my own hair that everybody I saw would say, "Oh, I see you cut your own hair."

But there are lots of things we can do ourselves instead of paying others to do them.

And you can certainly enjoy the savings—and the satisfaction of a job well done (hopefully).

– 19 –

Make things yourself instead of buying them

I am talking about everything from pizzas and marinades and salad dressings and breadcrumbs and baby food to drinks like tea and orange juice. I sometimes even make my own ice ahead when we are entertaining.

One of my pet peeves is the high-priced cut-up fruit that you see at the supermarket. I mean, come on, who is *not* able to cut up their own fruit? And who is it that pays big money for a jug of iced tea—when you can make a gallon that tastes better for just a few cents?

Do the math on making your own pizza versus ordering delivered pizza from one of the home-delivery places. Even if you buy ready-made crusts, or even frozen pizzas and add ingredients to them, you still come out way ahead—and it can be just as tasty or tastier—and actually hot right out of the oven.

Another thing you can make yourself are cleaners for windows, tubs, floors, toilets, and sinks. They are so easy to make and oh-so-cheap, and many are green to boot.

There are several core ingredients for making your own all-purpose green cleaners—baking soda, which is a deodorizer and an abrasive; white distilled vinegar, which is a disinfectant and a deodorizer; lemon juice, which is a disinfectant; and plain old H_2O. It cannot be simpler or cheaper.

And here are a couple of super-cheap recipes for more chemical-based all-purpose cleaners that will cost you pennies compared with the pricey array of cleaners you see at the supermarket.

All-purpose cleaner: ½ cup ammonia, ½ cup vinegar, and ¼ cup baking soda in a gallon of warm water.

Disinfectant spray: Mix ½ cup bleach and 3½ cups water. The total cost will be about a dime.

– 20 –
Don't smoke

Don't smoke. I know the price of cigarettes var-ies from state to state, but no matter where you are, it is an expensive habit—not to mention all of the troublesome health aspects of smoking. I used to be a smoker. In fact, I *loved* smoking so much that I can safely say I will *never* smoke again, because it was sooo, sooo hard for me to quit. Excruciating, tortur-ous, miserable. I mean, no one wanted to be anywhere around me during that dark withdrawal time.

It has been about 25 years since I kicked the habit, and I thought it might be fun to figure out how much money I've saved by quitting.

Thanks to a calculator on the www.cancer.org site's "Great American Smokeout" link, I determined that the cost of my cigs, based on the measly $1.50

a pack that I used to pay for my pack-a-day habit, would be $13,687.50.

Add to it inflation and today's new taxes, cigarettes now cost over $4 a pack, so we're talking about even more serious money—in the neighborhood of $38,000—if we calculate smoking a pack a day for 25 years starting now.

I'm not blowing smoke about this. A pack a day for 25 years is a lot of cigarettes (182,500), and $38,000 is a lot of money. As an MSN Money article concluded: "The financial consequences of lighting up stretch far beyond the cost of a pack of cigarettes. Smokers pay more for insurance. They lose money on the resale value of their cars and homes. They spend extra on dry cleaning and teeth cleaning. Long term, they earn less and receive less in pension and Social Security benefits."

Well, they say money talks. I'm hoping to convince you that quitting smoking can be your ticket not only to better health, better breath, and better-smelling clothes and home, but also to a substantial chunk of disposable income for you to spend on other things, such as trips or electronics, food or entertainment, or even a hefty down payment on a home.

Financial reasons to quit:

- Smoking a pack a day could cost you $1,511 a year.
- Smoking a pack a day could cost you $15,111 over 10 years.
- Health insurance for people who smoke increasingly involves a surcharge.
- MSN Money reports that a "40-year-old who quits and puts the savings into a 401(k) could save almost $250,000 by age 70."
- Think of all the fun and good things you could do with that money if you weren't spending it on nasty ol' smokes.

~ 21 ~

Be as energy efficient as possible

Be as energy efficient as possible—and always look for creative new ways to cut your usage—for the environment and for your pocketbook. Going green is not always cheaper but it often is.

Here are some tips for making your home more energy efficient:

• You can do your own energy audit online at www.energyright.com/savingenergy/evaluation.htm to find out how energy efficient your home is and what you can do to improve it.

• It would be nice to be able to heat your water more efficiently, since heating water is the second-biggest energy consumer in the home. You might consider changing to an energy-efficient water heater when the one you have needs to be replaced. In the meantime, changing the temperature setting to 120 degrees instead of the factory-set 140 degrees can save some serious dollars.

• Dishwashers don't use as much energy as you might think. More than 80 percent of the energy used by a dishwasher is for heating water. Use the lightest wash setting that will do the job. The heavy-duty settings use more water and, therefore, cost more.

• Refrigerators are the third-largest energy consumers in the home (behind space heaters and water heaters), accounting for 6 to 16 percent of a home's total energy cost. Refrigerators with freezers on top are more efficient than the side-by-side ones, which cost about $11 a month compared with $7 a month.

• Keep the fridge temperature between 36 and 38 degrees, with the freezer between 0 and 5 degrees. Anything lower will needlessly add to your energy cost. Other tips: a full fridge or freezer is more efficient than an empty one; don't put hot food directly into a refrigerator or freezer; and vacuum the coils every three months or so to keep the condenser running better.

• Fluorescent compact light bulbs are more efficient than the incandescent bulbs most of us use. They're expensive on the front end, but they can be worth it. The $6.97 75-watt bulb I saw at The Home Depot has a seven-year guarantee and claims to save up to $56 in energy costs per lamp. Plus, the package says it will last 13 times longer than standard bulbs. That's a bonus if you're like me and hate climbing a ladder to change bulbs.

• Ceiling fans can help you save in all seasons because they are so cheap to operate—using about 100 watts, which is just a little more than an average light bulb. In summer, you can set your thermostat at 80 and use a fan to make the room feel like 72 degrees. The air movement makes it feel cooler and allows you to raise the thermostat. In winter, in a room with high ceilings, running a fan on low can keep the heated air closer to the floor.

• Washers and dryers are energy vampires. To cut your usage, do full loads, use cold water whenever possible, and keep the lint filter clean. Also, if your dryer has a moisture sensor that automatically shuts off the unit when clothes are dry, use it. Or better yet, get a clothesline or rack for air drying.

• Conserve when you're not around. When you go out of town, turn the water heater off or way down. Most of us know this, but I wonder how many actually do it.

• And last but not least, in the cold months, get a sweater or sweatshirt and wear it—you'd be surprised at how that extra layer helps your comfort level at those lowered temps.

– 22 –

Order smart at restaurants

Order smart at restaurants. This is really easier than it sounds. Consider splitting items or ordering off the appetizer menu or ordering a combination of side dishes as an alternative to going with the full entrée. In places where the portions are always supersized, ask for a "to-go" box before you start eating and split the meal so that you can enjoy half in the restaurant and the other for another meal later. One of my readers says she routinely goes to a restaurant that has a big, wonderful salad bar that comes with the meal. She eats the salad bar offering in the restaurant and takes the untouched entrée home for the next night.

I do what I call "menu matching" with my family when we are on the road—for example, when we eat breakfast at Waffle House, my husband usually doesn't want his grits, so instead of ordering grits for myself, I ask the server to put my husband's portion in a bowl for me. I usually order coffee and at the end of the meal, I request a to-go cup of ice. I pour my leftover coffee in and add a little sweetener and have an iced coffee to go. It may sound too cheap for you, but to me it falls under the "waste not, want not" mantra.

If you can find restaurants that allow you to bring your own wine, you can enjoy some serious savings if you are a wine drinker. Honestly, lots of restaurants charge as much for a glass of wine as I pay for a whole bottle, and I'm talking about a 1.5 liter bottle.

It's also a good idea to check www.restaurant.com for some good savings at lots of restaurants.

Another money-saving trick is to eat your big meal at lunch, when it is usually cheaper than in the evening. And find restaurants that have early-bird specials to get a nice break.

So many cities have the *Entertainment* books (www.entertainment.com), which include hundreds of money-saving coupons for buy-one-get-one-free meals and other offers. There is a dinner club that I know about where each couple buys an *Entertainment* book and chooses a different restaurant from it each month for their two-for-one meal out.

It is also a good idea to buy one of the savings books for other cities (*Entertainment* has books on 150 markets) if you are traveling, since they have so many good offers on restaurants and attractions. These books, which cost $20 to $25, claim to have $16,000 worth of potential savings. Of course, not even the cheapest cheapster could use them to that extent, but even if you use 5 or 10 percent of the coupons, you are waaaay ahead of your $25 investment.

~ 23 ~
Change the way you entertain

Instead of going out, think of entertaining "in." There are lots of options. Instead of hosting a dinner party, put together a brunch—which can be a lot cheaper. Or even better, host a potluck where everybody brings a dish. Our neighborhood has an informal "happy hour" on scattered Friday nights where one couple or individual invites the crowd to their home, and everybody brings a bottle of wine and an appetizer. It is great fun—and no big burden on the host or guests, especially since it rotates from house to house.

You can also have a game night, where you play cards or Charades or board games like Scrabble or something new like Catch Phrase.

Or host a themed party, such as an auction party,

as a way to get rid of things you don't want and ac-quire things you do want. Ask each guest to bring at least one item they'd like to get rid of—anything from computers to jewelry, clothing, books, movies, plants, or whatever.

No matter what your theme, if everyone brings something to eat and what they are drinking, it is bound to be a super-affordable gathering for the whole crowd.

– 24 –
Use the library to the fullest

Everybody knows that the library has books, and most people know that libraries have movies and music for people to check out.

But these days, there is so much more. So find out what your library has and start taking advantage of what your tax dollars are paying for. Most libraries have fabulous programs for children and adults— not just story times and book readings, but marionette shows, workshops, musical shows, poetry sessions, book clubs, and more.

The interlibrary loan program allows you to borrow books from hundreds of other libraries if your library doesn't have what you want in its inventory.

There are often lots of resources for startup businesses and small businesses, and you can usually count on resourceful reference librarians who love to help you find whatever it is that you need.

Another library service people don't seem to know about are the fabulous free databases that you can have free access to through your library. Not all libraries are created equal, but I think you'd be pleasantly surprised if you checked your system. Our library has Auto Repair Center, Novelist (if you like this writer, try this one), Heritage Quest Online to do your family tree, and Health and Wellness Resource Center with reliable info on alternative medicine and nutrition.

You can log on to Value Line without paying, and you can take advantage of expensive-to-own study aids and home business–related materials, like Gale Virtual Reference Library (encyclopedias, almanacs, and specialized reference right from the desktop); Stat-USA (business info from the federal government); General OneFile (articles from thousands of scholarly, trade, and general interest publications, as well as Learning Express, which offers practice for the GED, ACT, SAT, and other tests.

– 25 –
Purchase used books

Before you spend money for more reading material, glance at your own bookshelves to see what treasures have remained unread. If you are like me, I'm willing to bet that there are some goodies there that you meant to read and would still love to read or if not, that you should sell or trade in for something more compelling.

There are wonderful used-book stores all over the country and most of them buy, sell, and trade books as well as music and movies. In most cases you pay half or less of the retail list price and then can resell them or trade them back in when you finish. There are lots of Web sites for buying, selling, and swapping books and other media. Some are www.half.com and of course www.amazon.com.

Most library systems also have regular book sales where they sell donated and surplus books as fund-raisers for library resources and programs.

Thrift stores like Goodwill and Salvation Army have wonderful books at great prices, and yard sales are also a good source for super-affordable reading material.

It is also fun to organize a book swap where everybody brings 5 to 10 books and trades them for 5 to 10 other books.

And if you're in school or have college students in your family, used textbooks are definitely the way to go. Buy them directly from other students or get the ISBN and buy them online at lots less than what most school bookstores charge.

— 26 —

Change the gift-giving rules for the holidays and other occasions

If you're ready to make a change, the best way to get the ball rolling is to speak up. I think you'll likely find that if you have determined that your gift giving has gotten out of hand, other people in your circle probably think so, too. Someone has to initiate the change and it might as well be you.

I've heard from so many families and groups of friends who found that they felt a sense of relief that they could just get together and enjoy one another's company instead of exchanging all of the unnecessary gifts.

There are lots of alternatives like drawing names, giving family gifts, trimming some names off your list altogether, just buying children's presents, and focusing on alternative gifts, such as services like babysitting, doing yard work, driving an elderly person to a doctor, making a special meal. There are tons of personalized options that the recipient would appreciate. I have even heard of a grandmother or aunt giving a coupon to a child for a special day out that they get to plan.

You may have to be creative in coming up with alternatives to the traditional give-till-it-hurts ritual, but it can work. I heard of one family that considered celebrating Valentine's Day—or even Christmas—a few days late in order to take advantage of the super after-holiday sales!

I don't think I could go that far, but seriously, just think how much nicer the holidays would be if the stress of aimless shopping was eliminated. And just think how nice it would be to know that the gifts you are giving would truly be appreciated and valued instead of being relegated to a closet or the attic.

– 27 –

Reevaluate your Christmas holiday traditions

Your goal should be to make the holidays a satisfying and meaningful time that suits your family's situation and values.

One tactic is to sit down with your family right after Christmas and go back over the holiday season. Determine what you and your family enjoyed and found to be worthwhile, and at the same time identify the things that were frustrating or over the top and the things that made you crazy.

Decide what kind of Christmas or holiday you want to have and what kind you can realistically deliver. And then make a pact with your family to make next year heavy on the good things and avoid the bad ones.

And then when next year comes, stick to your guns.

You should also figure out how much you spent on the holidays so that you will have a realistic point of reference next year.

– 28 –

Let people know what you want

At gift-giving time, I think it makes sense to let people know what you would like to have instead of their wasting time and money buying you stuff that will end up in the attic or basement or closet. For my birthday last year, I told my husband that I would love to have him take a ring he had given me to our jeweler to replace two stones that had gone missing. I loved it!

My brother told me about a belt that he really wanted for Christmas. It didn't sound too exciting, but it made so much more sense for me to get it than to look aimlessly around the mall and take a chance on getting something that he would never use.

Don't get me wrong, I love a good surprise too, but you can't always pull that off. Just think of the literally billions of dollars of well-intentioned but un-wanted gifts that are cluttering up people's storage areas.

– 29 –
Go for regifting

Go for regifting. Regifting—the practice of giving a person something that you received from someone else—is perfectly fine in my book, if it is done in the right spirit. Even Miss Manners says it's O.K.

Doing it *right* means giving someone something you have that you truly think they'd like. You don't give your best friend the ugly sweater or tacky earrings somebody gave you three years ago.

But you could give a pal the brand-new, still-in-the-box coffee grinder that your aunt gave you last year and you don't want because you already have one. Knowing where it came from shouldn't be important.

In some lights, regifting can be the most thoughtful way to give. For example, for a wedding gift, a friend's mother gave my husband and me a silver bread tray with an "H" engraved on it that had been in her family for two generations. She said nobody in her family ever knew what the "H" was for and that it must have been for Hance.

It wasn't that she was too cheap to buy us a "real" wedding gift, but more that she had something she honestly thought we'd like better than what she could buy. And we do love it.

So I say look around your closets, attic, and basement and see what you have that someone on your list would love. Wrap it up and give it without a tinge of guilt.

Regifting just gets a bad rap from people who take it too far, like the baseball team owner who sent a bouquet of "used" flowers to the umpires' association after the death of one of the umpires.

Knowing when to regift and when not to is crucial! So here are a few rules:

- Never regift items if you aren't sure what they

are, such as homemade canned foods someone gave you but you have no clue what it is.

• Never regift items if you're not sure how old the gift is, such as a box of candy that you found in a closet from an unknown Christmas past.

• Never regift items if you're not sure who gave them to you. The danger here obviously is that you might regift something to the same person who gave it to you to begin with!

• Always check to be sure there are no telltale signs (like a card or a note) that will give you away.

• Never regift an item just to get rid of it. The only time to regift is when you think the recipient will really like it.

− 30 −
Save on travel

There are lots of ways to save on travel, starting with checking your library for travel books, and doing lots of your research online.

Being flexible is crucial to getting the best vacation for the least amount of money. So pick a price, not a place, and go where the price is best.

Going off-season on vacation can mean big savings at almost every destination, too. Sometimes just one week makes a big difference in rates, so be flexible if you possibly can.

If you are booking a hotel room or a condo, be persistent and keep asking if there is a lower rate for AARP or AAA or corporate discount or student discount, or whatever else they may have that you are eligible for. It is also a good idea to call the hotel directly in addition to dealing with the corporate reservations folks, just in case they have a different offer. There is usually an 800 number to both.

I always try to stay in hotels that offer free breakfast—it's an especially good idea if you are traveling as a family with lots of hungry mouths to feed.

And I've known some resourccful readers to take a Crock-Pot along on trips to places like Disney World so that they can cook a cheap and healthful family meal in the hotel room while they are out enjoying themselves in the park and have dinner all ready when they return at mealtime.

I haven't done that myself, but when our girls were little, we did take a toaster and bread, bagels, and fruit so that we could have a cheap and easy—and leisurely—family breakfast in the room.

Traveling with another family is also a great idea—if, of course, you pick the right other family to spend your vacation with. When our children were growing up, the best (and cheapest) vacations were a drive to the beach. We would share a condo with our great friends David and Christy, whose daughters were about the same ages as ours and take turns cooking and watching the children. It was the perfect setup—having a little alone time and enjoying our family and group time, too. And the price was right—we shared the costs of the condo and food and other incidentals.

I'm not a camper, but I know that outdoor accommodations are a great way to go if you want to minimize costs. State parks have so much to offer and are super affordable and usually safe, not just for camping, but also for modest accommodations like cabins and basic inns.

There are also volunteer vacations and working vacations where you can get all or most of your expenses paid in exchange for your service. Sites like www.wildernessvolunteers.org are a good start.

And if you are older, the elderhostel.org site has tons of learning vacations that are priced right.

Whatever you do and wherever you go, take the time to do your research. For example, if you are going to a theme park, check the Web site and call the 800 number before you go to see what promotions they have coming up and if one time is better (cheaper) than another. There is nothing more frustrating than to arrive at the ticket office only to realize that if you had kcpt the empty Pepsi can that you just threw out at the rest stop that you could have saved $5 a ticket for your group. So always ask about the current deals before you make your move.

— 31 —

Consider a vacation in which you don't actually travel

In the current economy, where people have less and less disposable income for family vacations, more families are choosing what tourism officials have dubbed a "staycation," where you forgo the gas and motel costs and stay home to enjoy the attractions in your own backyard.

Most folks are surprised at what wonderful offerings their area has that they have never taken time to experience. Think about museums, restaurants, nature centers, parks, cultural venues for plays and concerts, historic home tours, botanical gardens, and so much more.

Here in Nashville where I live, you can easily fill a wonderful week visiting our attractions on the cheap, using coupon books and promotions and taking advantage of offerings that are free all the time.

No matter where you are, a good place to start is to contact your convention and visitors bureau and get their guides that list attractions and upcoming events. These are usually designed for tourists, but it's only right that you are a savvy tourist in your own town, too.

～ 32 ～
Go for automatic bill pay

Go for automatic bill pay on as many bills as possible. Most of these programs are free, and not only do you save the cost of postage—you also shouldn't have to worry about slipping up and getting hit with a late fee.

Don't think that "automatic" means foolproof. You still need to be diligent in checking your bills and making sure that everything is in order. "Automatic doesn't mean autopilot," says Curtis Arnold, founder of CardRatings.com. "You can't just set these payments up and let them cruise."

− 33 −
Negotiate

In a survey by the Consumer Reports National Research Center, the vast majority of people who haggled over the furniture, electronics, appliances, and even doctor bills said they had snagged at least one discount in the past three years. But in the same survey, 40 percent of respondents admitted that they rarely if ever even try to talk down a price. One in three women said they didn't haggle because they were worried about looking foolish. Well, get over it, because the age-old tactic of haggling actually works.

If you are going to haggle, there are a few things to be aware of. Be as nice as you can and don't ever be insulting. It is O.K. to offer less than the stated price, but be realistic in your offer and do it in a way that is not overaggressive or surly. The nicer you are, the better your chances are of getting what you want.

Volume discounts are a good way to go, so ask about buying three of whatever it is to get a better deal. And offer cash to improve your position—especially to independent retailers who are sometimes willing to give you a price break if you pay cash instead of using your credit card, since it costs them more to process a card transaction.

If you know there is a coupon but you don't have yours with you, always ask if they will honor it anyway—because they probably will. Some even honor competitors' coupons as well as their own. Bed Bath & Beyond is legendary for accepting expired coupons and for accepting competitors' coupons.

ShopSmart magazine offers these tips for haggler wannabes: Never buy anything without researching prices, never start with the price you are willing to pay, and don't give up.

― 34 ―

Don't waste your money on extended warranties

Don't waste your money on extended warranties. Consumer experts agree that the best strategy is to just say no. I read one recent article that said 80 percent of warranties go unused, so you're better off keeping your money.

One clever reader of mine said that instead of buying the extended warranties, he set up his own warranty fund, where he puts aside the amount that the company suggests in a special account and uses that when anything goes bad.

"It occurred to me when we were buying my daughter a stereo for Christmas that the price of the extended warranty was almost a quarter of the total price of the item. I put that money in a savings account and continued to do that with appliances, watches, cars, and anything where an additional warranty was offered," said Jerrie Barber of Nashville. "Now when something breaks, we take money from the fund and reimburse ourselves. We give good service to ourselves and we have never had trouble with a claim," he said, laughing. The "pay yourself" concept is a clever idea.

~ 35 ~
Enter contests

Enter contests. Oh, my gosh, can the super-serious contest enterers really rack up the prizes. I recently wrote about a Middle Tennessee lady named Greta Kirby who had won $50,000 worth of prizes in one year, including an all-expenses-paid trip to the Super Bowl, a brand-new car, and tons of other smaller goodies by entering online sweepstakes.

Before you tell me that it is all luck, you should know that this "lucky lady" spends three hours or so a day on the computer and enters 125 contests every single day. In other words, it can be a lot of work, but there are definitely payoff possibilities. To get started, check out www.sweepstakestoday.com or www.sweepstakesadvantage.com to find good, legitimate sweepstakes.

I have also written about some other contest winners—the duo Dianne Gregory and her daughter Julie Carter—who are obsessed with entering local contests and who both win all sorts of prizes all year long. They actually compete with each other to see which one—the mother or the daughter—can win the most stuff in one year. Their winnings are impressive to say the least—trips, computers, gift cards, a Wii Fit, TVs, free meals, and more.

I don't know if I could ever get into it the way these contest contessas have, but they are living proof that if you don't enter, you don't win! So enter and enter often to see if you can make your own luck.

~ 36 ~
Sign up for a membership

Memberships to attractions in your area can be a good way to go for family entertainment since they offer unlimited admission, and often guest privileges as well. One of the best tactics, if you have children, is to join a different attraction every year with your membership year running July 1 to June 30.

One year it might be the zoo and the next year the science center or art museum or some other family-friendly place. That way, your family can enjoy more than one attraction in the summer months and gain exposure to just about everything in your area over the course of several years. You'll be able to do it all, without the expense of joining everything at the same time.

And no matter what you join, be sure you know

what all the membership includes. Some membership include camp discounts, special gift shop deals, free parking, or deals for bringing guests. You might as well get all the perks if you are paying.

~ 37 ~
Volunteer

Volunteer. Not only are you doing some good, but there are often lots of perks for those willing to give their time and talents. For example, many theatrical and musical organizations seek volunteers to serve as ushers and greeters or perform other duties in exchange for free tickets to the events. The same goes for some college and professional sports. Other organizations reward volunteers with concert tickets, meals, and fun and interesting special events.

Volunteering is also a great way to meet people with similar interests and values, learn new skills, and be exposed to parts of your community that you might not otherwise experience on your own. One reader of mine learned all sorts of home improvement skills by being a regular Habitat for Humanity volunteer.

The added bonus is that if you are spending your time volunteering, you're not out shopping and spending money. And of course, if you volunteer, there is a wonderful satisfaction that comes from helping others.

– 38 –

Find ways to be cheap
to be generous

This may be my favorite tip, because I really do not believe in being cheap just to be cheap. If you can figure out ways to use your money-saving tactics to help others, all the better.

One of the best and most thoughtful tips ever to come across my desk was from a reader who said she had found a way to stretch her dollar with her Angel Tree participation. I'm sure you are all familiar with the Salvation Army Angel Tree, where you "adopt" a needy child and buy Christmas gifts for him or her.

Well, this fine lady, Ardyce House, told me that she starts buying gifts for a 14-year-old girl in January and then buys items on sale all year—spreading her spending over the months, and trolling for bargains for her targeted age group. By the time the

Angel Tree kiosks go up at the malls in October, she has enough stuff for four or five girls instead of the one or two she could have afforded if she had waited until the last minute. I had to ask, why the 14-year-old girl, and her answer was, "Oh, they are always the last ones picked from the Angel Tree because they are so hard to buy for." Isn't that great? Talk about being a good steward.

The same kind of forward thinking can go into buying food to donate to the local food bank. I mean, why not use your coupons or get the senior discount or whatever you can do to get as much food as possible for your money?

Another smart idea on the cheap to be generous is to give to schools through various grocery programs, where you sign up to support a particular school or charity, and the grocery gives a small percentage of your purchases to that group. You don't have to have school-age children to be able to sign up. It really is a great, free way to help our schools.

I've also heard of lots of folks who have what they call "parties with a purpose"—say a birthday party or anniversary gathering or bar mitzvah, where instead of bringing gifts for the honoree(s), guests bring food for the food bank, or children's books for a literacy organization, or stuffed animals for the children's hospital.

There is a bonus in all of this generosity, too—you can often make it count in your favor at tax time, when you can take a deduction for what you have given.

− 39 −
Never turn down anything free

If you can't use it, you can probably find someone who can. A great example is the little bottles of lotion, shampoo, and other products that you find in hotels. They are great for homeless shelters, nursing homes, and other spots that need individual products. If you go to a convention and they give away pens, you may not need or want them, but you can always give them to your favorite charity's office.

Every little bit helps, so be on the lookout all the time for freebies. Free food can go to the food bank, and miscellaneous items can always be donated to area thrift shops for them to sell. Or, if you are having a garage sale, slap a price tag on the freebie and see what you can get for it.

A great source for freebies is www.freecycle. org—a nationwide site where people list things they want to give away.

– 40 –

Take advantage of cheap or free greeting cards

Take advantage of cheap or free greeting cards. It's crazy what people spend on all-occasion cards when they don't have to spend much of anything. Here are some of my ways to get around this expense.

Write a note. Seriously, a hand-written note can be so much more meaningful than some trite card. You can go to a stationery store and buy the nicest card stock or notepaper for the same price as three or four forgettable ready-made cards.

You can also reuse the pretty cards that people have sent to you. This may sound extreme, but there are actually several clever ways to do it.

The easiest is to cut the cards down the seam and save the pretty part to use as a postcard. Not only is it essentially a free card, but you also get the cheaper postcard postage. Several smart readers say they have used one year's Christmas cards as the next year's Christmas postcards. It's really not a bad idea.

If you want a "real" card as opposed to a postcard, you can glue the pretty part onto card stock to make a new card.

My mother (we call her "Queen Cheap") used to send me a nice, expensive card and write a personal note to me on a sticky note so that I could resend the unsigned card to someone else. (I have learned a lot from my mother, believe me!)

Her other trick that I thought was worth sharing was that she gave my daddy the same Valentine card every year. He would look at it and say, "That's nice," and set it down. As soon as he scurried off to work, she would slip it back in her dresser drawer and save it for the following year. After he died, we never knew whether he knew it was the same card or if he just didn't say anything because he was proud of her for being so cleverly thrifty. I guess we will never know. I have also heard of people who found the perfect card for a friend or brother or sister and sent it back and forth between each other on the designated occasion year after year.

And then this, from one of my readers, an award-winning cheapster named Howard Suiter: "Greeting cards for loved ones have become very expensive. I grocery shop with my wife to ensure that we don't spend too much and during our trip to Kroger, I went to the birthday card section and selected three lovely and expensive cards while my wife searched for bargains. I then let my wife read the cards, wished her a happy birthday, and then returned the cards, unharmed, to the rack. My wife said I was really 'cheap.' The selection I made must have been memorable because she has never forgotten that birthday."

And if you just have to buy cards, it is nice to know that Dollar General, Big Lots, Dollar Tree, and other stores have some that are two for a dollar, which is not bad.

And of course there are lots of Web sites where you can send e-cards for free—like www.bluemountain.com, 123greetings.com, and www.regards.com.

- 41 -

Be frugal on the gardening front

I love plant swaps—where everybody brings perennials or other plants to trade for other people's garden material. It is a great way to start your landscaping or a garden and a great way to clear out crowded beds.

Another great money-saver is to keep seeds from one year to the next and to start your own plants—literally for pennies.

If you are new to gardening and want instant success, my advice is start with a small herb garden—either in the ground or in a container like a large planter or barrel. Not only is it incredibly easy to grow herbs like basil, oregano, mint, and rosemary, but growing your own can be a huge savings if you use many herbs in your cooking.

If you want proof, just go to the grocery and price

one of those little packs of fresh basil or other herbs in the produce section. Then compare it with the cost of growing one plant that produces a mound of basil over the course of the summer, and you will be instantly and solidly sold on the concept of herb gardening.

Another great tip on the gardening front is to take full advantage of the resources of your state or county's agricultural extension service. These agents know *everything* from how to evaluate your soil, to what to do about bugs or diseases on your plants, to tips on the best way to grow tomatoes or other vegetables or flowers.

And like almost everything, it is good to have a sense of humor. A really funny tip that came my way in one of my "cheap" contests was from a lady who said she had two spruce trees in pots on her patio that died. Rather than buy new ones, she bought a 99-cent can of outdoor spray paint in a "natural looking green color" and sprayed them. She said they seemed to last forever, and she never even had to water them.

~ 42 ~

Keep a gift closet for storing "all-purpose" gifts

Keep a gift closet. Then you can look for bargains all year, instead of having the last-minute pressure to come up with something for a birthday, or hostess gift. Having the stocked closet also curbs the aggravating tendency to overspend on a last-minute gift because you just don't have time to really look around. Busy parents with young children who are faced with the almost weekly birthday party schedule are the best beneficiaries of the stocked-up bargain gift closet because they will be ready with age appropriate birthday presents at a minimum cost no matter when the invitation arrives.

It's important to take inventory every now and then so that you don't overstock.

– 43 –
Be skeptical

If it seems too good to be true, it probably is. This is one tip that will serve you well in so many areas of your life. There are lots of gimmicks out there, and with this economy, there is an increasing number of scams, and they seem to get more sophisticated all the time. So be on your guard and take your time before you act on anything that seems sketchy. Good resources for checking things out include the Better Business Bureau and the Department of Consumer Affairs for your state.

~ 44 ~
Go halfsies

A lot of cheapos enjoy splitting meals at restaurants to save, but I hear about other less-obvious things that you can cut in half, without compromising much. Think dryer sheets, paper towels, paper napkins, Popsicles, candy bars (a whole Hershey is really too much for most folks), even dog biscuits. You might even try half the detergent in the dishwasher or washing machine.

My mother used to make my brother and me split a piece of gum (Juicy Fruit) partly because she was cheap, but perhaps more because she was afraid we would swallow it and half of a stick would be less bad for us than a whole one.

Some halfsies make more sense than others. I've heard of people who cut Band-Aids in half lengthwise to make them a better, slimmer fit for a certain hard-to-protect sore spot. And the cheapest thing I've heard on the halfsies front was a man who said he broke a toothpick in half so that he and his wife could share one, instead of using two. Uggh. That is just too cheap!

– 45 –

Stay home more

Moneysavingmom.com says, "My number one tip for keeping things simple and saving money is to stay home more. Staying home is one of the simplest ways to have more time, spend less money, accumulate less clutter, and well, to plain just live a less frantic lifestyle."

How true!

I recently wrote about an older couple in Middle Tennessee who say they only leave home twice a week—to attend church on Wednesday and Sunday—and that their grocery shopping is done on the way to or from church. That's pretty extreme, and I'm not close to promoting something this radical, but it is abundantly clear that staying home and staying away from the tempting stores saves you money and gives you time to do all sorts of constructive things.

– 46 –
Stay out of the stores

I often tell people that my best money-saving tip is "Don't go shopping." I know it sounds oversimplistic, but I can tell you that it is very effective. If you don't go, you don't spend. The malls and merchants are good at what they do, and their goal is to get you to buy something you didn't know you needed, or sometimes things you didn't even know existed.

So many of us just go out shopping, almost as a hobby, and say it is "just to look." Well, you know the chances are overwhelming that you will find something out there to buy. Impulse buying is clearly what drives retail, so stay away if you can.

– 47 –

Talk to your children and grandchildren about money

I read this great quip in the paper: "Money is like sex, if you don't talk to your children about it, they'll learn about it from their friends." And that is not good. Your good example and your teachable moments can go a long way toward steering your children to become responsible and accountable consumers.

If you need to cut back, I think it is a great idea to get the whole family involved in your reduced spending plan. But I also think it is important to approach in a positive and can-do way. Tell your family how and why things will be changing for a while. Have everyone think about ways they can help, and try to make it a team adventure. I'm not talking about saddling your young children with your budget woes, but getting everyone in on the plan can really help, especially if you are upbeat about it.

– 48 –
Make the most of your education

This is so fundamental, but it is crucial. Just look at the numbers: When students drop out of high school, they earn $7,000 less per year and $260,000 less over their lifetime, according to a report by the Alliance for Excellent Education.

A college master's degree is worth $1.3 million more in lifetime earnings than a high school diploma, according to a recent report from the Commerce Department's Census Bureau. The report reveals that over an adult's working life, high school graduates can expect, on average, to earn $1.2 million; those with a bachelor's degree, $2.1 million; people with a master's degree, $2.5 million; and those with doctoral degrees, $3 million.

So stay in school and learn all you can, so you can earn all you can.

– 49 –

Pay full price (every now and then, it's O.K.)

There is an exception to every rule—even the stalwart "never pay full price for anything" rule. Here is a tactic that one of my readers shared for those rare times when you feel compelled to pay full price. "If you have searched the world over for something and finally find it, and it is full price, go ahead and buy it, especially if you think you may never find it again. But be sure you know the store's return policy and then take it home, keep it in the package with tags and receipt, and watch the ads in the paper or call the store at regular intervals to see if it goes on sale. If it drops, head back over there and return the original one and then buy it—or its twin—back at the better price." If not, I say just enjoy it and go on, and make up the savings somewhere else.

– 50 –
Be patient

I've heard people say that today's fashion is tomorrow's Goodwill merchandise, and there is a lot of truth to that. If you need something but aren't in a hurry, it will eventually turn up at a garage sale, estate sale, or on eBay, or at the very least on sale at a retailer. So why not exercise patience and let someone else shell out the big bucks and then wait until the price is right.

The idea is to change the way we think about things—realizing that we don't have to have everything right now. We live in what author Ellie Kay calls an "add water and stir world" in which we "can get things when we want them, how we want them, without waiting."

It's called delayed gratification—and it is not just

for grownups. I think patience may be even more important for children, because they need to develop skills for planning and control. Yes, indeed, patience is a virtue.

– 51 –

Enjoy things that are good
to the last drop

I believe in saving every last drop of almost every-thing. I mean, when that ketchup bottle or mayon-naise jar seems empty, it really has a lot of content left inside. It is remarkable what a good spatula can scrape out.

Or take the liquid-laundry-detergent bottle, which I rinse repeatedly and add the watery suds to a load before throwing the bottle away. I add a little water to the last vestiges of my liquid soap and get another few days worth from my dispenser. My lotion bottle stands upside down as do my makeup and shampoo containers. Some cheapsters cut open their toothpaste tubes and glean a little extra for a few more brushings before they toss them. You may laugh, but why not use every bit? You paid for it, you know.

– 52 –
Consider a "fiscal fast"

Jeff Yeager, known as the "ultimate cheapskate," coined the "fiscal fast" phrase, where you spend no money for a prescribed period of time. You can start with one day of absolutely no spending on anything. Or you can be more ambitious and go for a week, which is what Yeager recommends. He also suggests getting the whole family in on the fast and trying to make it fun, like a game. The rules are pretty simple: no spending, keep the wallet shut. And he says no hoarding or stockpiling on the front end either.

Most folks are surprised at how well they can get by—when they see that they have food on hand, that shelter is available, and that transportation can probably be worked out with a carpool or bike or the gas you already have in the car. And as Yeager says, "If you can't go a week without buying clothes, you have a serious spending problem."

~ 53 ~

Take things back

Honestly, I will take almost anything back, if I change my mind or if there is a problem with something I bought.

Let's say I get home and the fresh strawberries I bought at the grocery turn out to be moldy at the bottom. I will definitely return them and get my money back. Sometimes calling the store will do the trick, and all you have to do is stop by customer service and collect on your next visit.

Or let's say, you get home from the mall and see that the skirt that you bought from a sale rack that advertised another 30 percent markdown, rang up at the higher price. I will go right back and settle up.

The point is, don't let the opportunity pass. You work too hard for your money to overpay or not get the product you were promised, and most businesses want you to be satisfied. But keep those receipts for sure—if you want to be a successful returnista.

− 54 −

Enjoy high school sports and theater

This is particularly appealing to parents who want to expose their children to competitive sports and live performances at affordable prices. The price of admission to high school basketball, soccer, and football games is usually minimal and sometimes even free. It is the same with high school theater and dance at many public and private schools. The price is usually right, and the shows are often surprisingly wonderful. And schools love a full house.

– 55 –
Attend leisure activities at local colleges

Take advantage of the offerings of the colleges and universities in your area. Most of them have wonderful (and affordable) theater, dance, and musical performances, competitive sports, lectures, lifelong learning opportunities, and beautiful campuses to visit just for the fun of it. The campuses are also a good place to look if you need some affordable extra help around the house, since students are usually looking to make a little spending money by babysitting, running errands, doing yard work, providing computer help, and offering other services.

Avoid clothes that need to be dry-cleaned

S teer clear of clothes that need to be dry-cleaned—
or at least seek out the cheap dry cleaners. My favorite story on this subject is about the $3.99 Jones New York pea-jacket that I bought at Goodwill on half-price day. I left the coat on our front porch to air out, planning to take it to my cheap one-price dry cleaners. Meanwhile, my sweet husband (who by the way is not cheap) saw the coat and decided to be nice and took it to his full-priced dry cleaner. When he returned to pick it up, the dry-cleaning price was over $12—three times more than I paid for the coat. Go figure.

I really try to avoid items that must be dry-cleaned and have found that some of them can be washed in cold water using Woolite (or the store-brand equivalent), with excellent results. Dryel, the product that dry-cleans in your home dryer, is another option. I heard from a mom with two high school band students, that Dryel worked well on repeated treatments for the band uniforms and saved her tons of money.

And if you just must take your things to a professional full-price dry cleaner, shop around for prices and deals and look for coupons and volume discounts. There are some discounters that require that you pay when you drop your clothes off and give you a price break. And some offer volume deals where, if you bring in ten or more items at a time, you get a better deal.

– 57 –

Shop your own closet

Shop your own closet. They say that most people only wear 25 percent of what is in their closets— so why not expand your horizons? The first step is to take an inventory of your wardrobe—and get rid of things that don't fit, don't look good, or don't have any chance of being worn. Then organize what is left in a way that you know exactly what you have and which will mix and match.

If you have a fashionista friend, ask him or her to come in and help you look at your "inventory" with fresh eyes. Once you are organized, make a plan and work toward buying fewer but perhaps nicer clothes.

— 58 —
Host a clothing swap

Have a clothing swap where everyone brings a certain number of wardrobe items. You can include clothes, shoes, accessories, jewelry, and handbags, and simply let everyone do some swapping as an alternative to shopping. This is recycling at its best.

One of these exchanges took place in our area recently, where 75-100 ladies each brought between two and five items to swap and each one paid a $5 participation fee that was donated to a local charity. If you brought four things, you were given four tickets so that you could take home four items. Simple, simple, simple, and everybody leaves with something "new." The last thirty minutes of this particular sale was a free-for-all of all of the items that were left. A swap really is a great way to clean out and a great way to clean up, if you are lucky.

Shop consignment stores

Consignment shopping for clothes is a great way to get top brands for a fraction of the cost. Most cities now have lots of ladies' and children's sales and shops and a few men's consignment shops where you can take the gently used clothes and accessories that you no longer want.

It really is a wonderful form of recycling—and everybody wins, since shoppers get a bargain, sellers recoup some of their investment, and a small business thrives.

There are some things that you need to know on both sides of the equation. First are my tips for consignment shoppers:

• Shop often.

• Most shops have a "wish list" where you can tell them what you're looking for, and if that item comes in, they'll contact you.

• Get on the shop's e-mail newsletter list or mailing list so that you can be contacted about special sales or new inventory.

• Get to know the shop's owners and workers. I find that they want to help you and are happy to let you know when things you like come in.

• E-mail the shop and ask about specific things you're looking for.

• If you find merchandise that you like and that fits well, find out who the consignor is so you can ask specifically for his or her pieces.

• The only downside to being on the shopping side of the equation is that most of the stores have an "all sales final" policy, so be sure you really like and will wear what you're buying.

Tips for consignors with items to sell:

• Find out if you need an appointment before you

load up all your stuff.

• Find out what the split is. Some stores are 50-50, but some are 60-40 or even 70-30, with the store getting the lion's share.

• Know when the earliest take-in time is. The longer your items are on the floor, the more likely they are to sell.

• Know how they pay, whether they mail checks or whether you have to pick the check up.

• Ask about hidden fees.

• Be selective about what you bring; most shops want only items that are still in season.

• Make your items as presentable as possible— clean, pressed, and so forth.

• Ask how they price and whether you have any say-so in the pricing.

• Know that, in most cases, the shop is not responsible for your things in case of fire, flood, or other misfortune.

• Have a plan for your things that don't sell. Most shops give you the option of donating them or picking them back up at the end of the season.

— 60 —

Take advantage of all the great Web sites for cheapos

There are lots of good shopping and comparison sites, such as www.shopping.com, www.mysimon.com, www.shopping.yahoo.com, and www.pricegrabber.com. You can sort by price, and the sites let you search by products, retailers, or individual sellers. Here are some more good prospects:

• www.retailmenot.com is a great site for searching for codes to save you on just about anything at tons of stores. You just type in the Web address of the store you want to shop, and if there is a code, you've got it. Savvy shoppers consult the site to see if there is a coupon code before they buy almost anything.

• www.couponchief.com tries to make coupon searching easier and more efficient. There is even an online tutorial to help people learn to use the site.

• www.smartbargains.com is a bargain-hunting site.

• www.fatwallct.com is a rebate site where you can get money back for some of your purchases. The site gets a commission for linking you to participating retailers and then shares a little of that with you. The site has deals and tips.

• www.dealcatcher.com is a site offering print-able coupons and rebates at lots of stores, including Sephora and Omaha Steaks.

• www.insweb.com is recognized as a good ro source for getting quotes on all kinds of insurance. It consults 6,400 agents representing 21 companies.

• www.gasbuddy.com tells you where the cheapest gas is. Of course, it isn't really worthwhile to drive all over town for a few pennies in savings, but some-times the difference can be compelling. The rule of thumb is that unless you save more than a nickel per gallon and will be buying ten gallons or more, it is probably not worth making a trip out of your way.

- www.indexcreditcards.com compares the plethora of credit cards and their rewards. There are low interest cards, rewards cards, student cards, prepaid cards, and so on.

- www.overstock.com lists good discounts on clothes, housewares, books, music, and other items.

- www.factcheck.org has little to do with being cheap, but I just like to visit it for getting answers and checking the fact of the day.

- www.rather-be-shopping.com is a good place to look for coupons and deals.

- www.half.com is an eBay page with books, music, movies, textbooks, and more.

- www.buzzillions.com has thousands of product reviews.

- www.annualcreditreport.com allows you to request a free credit-file disclosure, commonly called a credit report, once every 12 months from each of the nationwide consumer credit reporting companies—Equifax, Experian, and TransUnion.

- www.couponmom.com has lots of printable coupons, coupon codes, free offers, free samples, and a blog that has lots of good information. It's one of my favorites.

- www.lastminute.com is a good site for last-minute travel.

- www.ebates.com is a site where you can shop with 900 merchants and get rebates that you can keep or donate to charity. You have to join, but it doesn't take long.

- www.mycoupon.com has tons of coupons for the grocery and restaurants.

- www.supercouponing.com is based in the Chicago area but has lots of good ideas.

- www.totallyfreecrap.com and www.heyitsfree.net both have all sorts of free stuff from screwdrivers to magazines and lip gloss and Nicoderm patches.

- www.freeshipping.org is a good one to check whenever you are buying anything online.

~ 61 ~
Google everything

If you like to shop online, always look for codes. Google the company and then type in "promotion code" or "rebate" or "coupon" or "free shipping" in addition to the site name you're planning to buy from. This can help you save lots of money, just by entering a code at checkout, or submitting a form by email. Taking the time to do a little extra search-work before purchasing can definitely pay off in online shopping. You can sometimes even "stack" codes—meaning you can use more than one on one product.

~ 62 ~
Learn what you can do without

In other words, think about what you are paying for that you are not really using. Are you really taking advantage of all those channels on your cable TV? Are you reading all the magazines that you subscribe to? Can you read your newspaper online instead of paying for a subscription? Can you rely solely on your cell phone and ditch the landline? Do you really have to have a haircut every four weeks or can you go a little longer? These are all good questions to ask yourself periodically, with an eye toward cutting back at least a tiny bit. Every little bit helps.

– 63 –
Use toll-free numbers

I know that everything has turned to the Internet and Web sites, but I still find toll-free numbers to be a good resource for people who still have landlines—and almost every company has one. I have heard from lots of readers who call company 800 numbers to ask if they have any samples or coupons for their products. The toll-free numbers are easy to find on the company's Web site or on products themselves.

Going the 800 number route is also often a more promising avenue for getting a problem resolved if you have the patience to go through all of the machinations and voice-activated prompts.

I use them for comparison purposes for hotel rates (call the central 800 number and the individual property's 800 number, too), and if you are going to an attraction like a theme park or museum, I find it is a good idea to look online and then make the 800 call to be sure there are no other promotions or deals other than what the Web site features.

— 64 —

Don't spend a lot of money on the movies

If you haven't noticed lately, a date night or family outing to the movies can be an expensive undertaking. Even renting movies or subscribing to Netflix can add up. So why not go cheaper with Redbox, or even better, check movies out of your local library. Our library system here in Nashville offers more than 50,000 VHS and DVD movies that you can take out for seven days, prepaid with tax dollars and free of extra charge, and I suspect wherever you live that your library has an impressive collection, too.

Redbox's $1 movies are also a great deal. There are more than 9,000 of the red kiosks in 48 states— mostly in supermarkets, drugstores, and McDonald's. I hear that Tuesday is the best day to go, since it is new-release day, and you can even reserve the movie you want by going to www.redbox.com.

Another cheap option is www.hulu.com, which has free movies that you can watch on your computer.

And if you just have to go to the theater, find out how much matinees can save you, or look for discounted theaters or tickets through your employer or stores like Costco or through AAA if you are a member.

– 65 –
Lower your standards

Be willing to lower your standards, even if just by a little bit. I'm not talking about ethical standards, I am talking about compromising your "champagne" tastes. The trick is not to make a barebones sacrifice of all that is good in your life, but rather to be willing to make some tradeoffs in some areas in order to have the things you *really* want in others.

The first step would be to experiment with a few "lesser things" and see what you think. Instead of a Dooney & Bourke bag, go with a knockoff. Instead of going for the expensive coffees every morning, start brewing a pot at home. Instead of a full manicure or pedicure, go with a polish change. Or maybe buy an 8 megapixel camera instead of a 12 megapixel one.

If you drink a lot of wine, consider the box wines

or 1.5-liter bottle bargains for some serious savings. Or if you are a beer drinker, drop back from Budweiser or Heineken to something cheaper like Natural Light.

There are lots of opportunities on the food front, too. Buy the bag of apples instead of individual apples. And if you are a name-brand nut, shift to a generic or store brand at least for some things, like maybe bread or crackers. Honestly, you may not be able to tell the difference, except in what you are saving.

Be creative in trying to find ways to have what you want, but at a lesser cost.

There's a catering company in my neighborhood that has this fabulous grilled shrimp that is just to die for, but obscenely expensive. I figured out really quickly that I couldn't afford much of it but that I could buy shrimp on sale at my grocery and persuade my husband to grill it similarly. Or if I just absolutely had to have the caterer's version, I could make a nice green salad and top it off with one or two of the grand shrimp per person and be satisfied at a fraction of the cost of serving a plateful.

There really are a lot of ways to be content for less. I loved this idea from a reader who shared this clever way her sweetie managed to be romantic and cheap all at once: "Buy seven roses instead of 12 and write on the card: 'You deserve a rose for every day of the week.'"

~ 66 ~
Compare prices on everything

There is really no excuse not to compare prices. It is so easy with the Internet and its various comparison sites and eBay.

Comparison shopping is something lots of cheapos do religiously, but one of my readers helped me see that you can kick it up a notch and apply it more broadly—to everything, including dentistry. She found a dentist who charges $40 for an exam, $65-$75 for cleanings, $90 for X-rays, and $150-$225 for fillings. That's compared with others who charged $50-$65 for an exam, $80-$375 for cleanings, $95-$110 for X-rays, and $170-$295 for fillings. Don't be afraid to shop for a deal in all areas of your life. It definitely can pay off. So think about comparing veterinarian fees, costs of particular prescriptions, hair salons, oil changes. I mean everything—large and small.

Taking the time to know your prices will prevent you from falling for a deal that is not really a deal at all.

— 67 —
Think ahead

Have you ever heard the expression "she had everything in dying order"? Don't laugh—it is the way we all should be just in case something happens, because *something* inevitably will happen. We all need to have a will, we need to have health-care power of attorney, we need a living will, and if we want to make it super easy for our survivors, we need a written plan of what we will like done at our funeral. It is not fun to talk about, but it is so important emotionally and financially for those we love.

– 68 –
Think multipurpose

Readers of my column are always coming up with clever ways to use items they have on hand for multiple purposes.

One smart mom said she bought a child's wagon to use as a basinet for her baby (the mattress is a perfect fit), knowing that when the baby got older, the wagon could be used in many other wonderful ways. Another reader used a large road atlas as a sun screen in her car, and another said she used a rolling pin for her exercising in place of a TV-promoted Abmaster— "It's the same motion," she told me.

Another said she uses a strand of spaghetti in place of those long matches when she needs to light her stove or pilot light, and yet another told me that when you don't have a proper stopper that you can put a golf ball in the sink or tub and it will hold water.

Pretty clever!

Here are some others:

Newspapers: Everybody knows that newspaper is good for cleaning windows and that it is fun to wrap presents in the comics, but there are lots of other uses—wrapping fish, lining bird cages, wiping up spills, safely packing material for breakables. But did you know that if you have to pick your green tomatoes when the frost hits, you can wrap each tomato in a couple of layers of newspaper and preserve them so that they'll ripen almost naturally?

Paperclips: I use a paperclip for a bookmark on my books, but there are lots of other uses. To get the last dab of toothpaste out, you can clamp the tube with a large clip and push up. They also hold pleats together if you are ironing, and you can open them up and use them as ornament hangers at Christmas.

Pillowcases: They are versatile—you can use one over your clothes to store them off-season in the closet. They are also great for storing old linens and leather or suede items like handbags or shoes. And king-sized pillow cases are conveniently just the right size to cover the pad on a baby's changing-table. You can also make easy, fun costumes out of them for the kiddos by painting them, cutting holes for the head and arms, and then adding a belt and other accessories.

Pizza cutters: They are not just for pizza anymore. They are great when trying to create manageable child-sized bites of everything from spaghetti to pancakes. You can also use them to cut green onions or to easily cut a Popsicle in half. I've even heard that the thin ones do a good job of loosening painted-shut windows.

Shower caps: They are handy for lots of jobs in addition to keeping your hair dry when showering. Vicki Lansky of *Family Circle* suggests wearing one when you are painting (especially ceilings) to keep the paint out of your hair. You can also slip a cap over the bottom of hanging plants before watering them, to catch the drips. And they make great food covers for items you are transporting.

Shower curtains and plastic tablecloths have many

lives. They are great as a protective layer on beds, under plants, and on other things that you want to protect. A friend uses a plastic tablecloth on her couch when she is not home so that her precious dog won't leave hair and other unmentionables on the furniture. They also make good drop cloths.

Products like Scrubbing Bubbles and the store brand equivalent are not just for bathroom cleaning. They are great for cleaning tennis shoes, tires, lawn furniture, and lots of other things.

And what about those little silica gel packages that come inside new shoes and other things you buy, that you usually just throw out? Well, they are actually useful. As desiccants, they keep moisture out and keep metals from tarnishing, so drop one in with your jewelry, or put a few packets in your toolbox to ward off the rust.

Why buy a bunch of new stuff when things you have around the house might work just as well?

– 69 –
Churches rock

Check out the churches in your area for community events. There are concerts, affordable meals, children's programs, Vacation Bible Schools, athletic teams, movies, and educational and social programs.

If you haven't noticed, churches are offering an increasing number of wonderful and sometimes unexpected programs. One church in our area has a climbing wall, another has a super-affordable fitness center. Churches invite the public to a growing number of helpful offerings like Dave Ramsey's *Financial Peace* workshops and classes on organizing, time management, and even cooking and gardening. Many churches have programs for seniors, counseling services for individuals and couples, and food pantries and thrift shops—all under the umbrella of outreach.

I also hear from travelers who scope out churches on their trips. They take advantage of fish fries, spaghetti suppers, and the like for affordable meals for the whole family. Not only do they get some great meal deals, but they also get to know the vaction spot from a local perspective.

– 70 –
Get that company match

If your employer matches all or part of your 401(k) contribution, milk it for all it's worth. Otherwise you are turning away free money. The typical large-company plan matches 50 percent of your contributions, up to 6 percent of your salary. Your match may not be as generous, but it still makes sense to take maximum advantage of what essentially is free.

Each dollar you don't put into a company retirement plan is subject to federal, state, and local income taxes. So if you're in a 30 percent combined (federal and state) tax bracket, each pretax dollar you plunk into your 401(k) should cost you only 70 cents.

– 71 –
Make the savings fun

If you can make the savings a challenge instead of a chore, you have more than half the battle won, and there are lots of fun ways to shrink your budget. Here are several fun ideas for shrinking your spending that my resourceful penny-pinching readers have shared with me over the years:

• Dollar devaluation: Jane Gault of Murfreesboro, Tennessee, and her cousin invented this game to motivate themselves to wear the clothes that are pushed to the back of a closet.

"You buy an item like a sweater for $15 and each time you wear it, subtract $1 until it is devalued to free status. Psychologically, it helps me to use things I have and not buy things that are too expensive. Who would want to wear a $100 sweater 100 times?"

• Shop and drop: Patti Miller of Nashville says when she has a shopping urge, she goes to Walmart. "We take a shopping cart and put anything we want in it for ten minutes. Then we take everything back to its spot and have a good high of 'no debt.'"

• Take a year off: My friend Susan had decided she was a shopaholic and had the maxed-out credit cards to prove it. So she decided to challenge herself to not shop for clothes, shoes, or accessories for an entire year. At the end of her moratorium, not only had she paid off her credit cards, but she said she also had a completely different perspective on shopping. She said she of course knew how much it cost to shop, but had never thought about how much time it took—and she said that her shopping fast had helped her see how much more time she had to do more productive things.

Oh, and she said the rudest awakening was that nobody seemed to notice. "All that time I had been thinking that everyone was saying, 'Look how cute Susan looks,' and nobody noticed."

• The great pretender: Judy Cummings of Cumberland Furnace, Tennessee, started using "pretend spending" as a way to save when she and her husband were preparing to adopt a baby. In the six months they had between the time they found out about the baby and when the baby arrived, they managed to save $4,000 with this strategy: "We would say, 'Let's go out to eat,' and then we would figure out what we normally spent on a meal out, including tax, and we would subtract that from our checkbook and write in 'special little account.' Then we would curl up on the couch with a couple of sandwiches and watch TV. It was surprising how easy it became to do." In more recent years, they have used the same "pretend to spend" strategy to fund a fantastic family cruise.

• Have a contest: Several families in a neighborhood with similar-sized houses held a contest to see which one could have the lowest combined light, gas, and water bill each month. The first few months the bills were almost identical and then all of a sudden, one family had a significantly lower tally. What had happened was the mom and dad were getting up super early and loading the kiddos into the car and heading to the local Y for all their showers. Not a bad idea.

• Lock-down: My friend Ann wanted living room furniture but didn't want to go into debt. So instead of putting the furniture on a credit card or some other payment program, she took a picture of the furniture and plastered it on her fridge door and her pantry door and proclaimed what she called "lock-down" in her kitchen, which meant that she could not go to the grocery until everything was gone. I mean everything, everything in her pantry, her refrigerator, and her freezer.

Yes, most of us stockpile to some degree and have a good bit of usable stuff just sitting there waiting. Ann said her "lock-down" worked out great—helping her fund her furniture and at the same time see that what she had for dinner was not *that* important.

Our family has used "lock-down" several times on the week or two before a vacation—just eating what is on hand and not going to the store—in order to free up a little extra money for our trip. It really is a good way to clean out and liberate some funds at the same time.

― 72 ―

If you or your spouse is a senior, go for that senior discount

Virtually every business has some sort of offer, but many of them do not post these offers.

Several deals kick in at 50, some at 60, 62, or 65. But it is up to you to ask, because most employees are not going to ask you if you are an oldster.

Many groceries have regular senior days during which you can save 5 to 10 percent off the top, which can definitely add up if you shop smart on those days and buy the things you need every month like toilet paper, dishwasher soap, and so forth. Using your coupons in conjunction with the discount kicks your savings up another notch.

Many major retailers and most movie theaters have senior days or senior offers, but it is up to you to know the details and do the asking.

People tend to think about senior deals being at restaurants and groceries and department stores, or maybe hotels and concerts, but many service companies have them, too. For example, if you are getting estimates on having a new heat-and-air unit installed, ask if the company offers a senior discount. If you are buying tires or getting an oil change, or just about anything else, ask.

And if you are not a senior but your spouse is, ask if you can get the discount in their name since you are a couple.

~ 73 ~
Let the kids eat free

Take advantage of the restaurant "kids eat free" deals. Tons of restaurants offer this—and it definitely can be a good deal. But be sure you know what you are getting into, because most of the deals come with some conditions, like you get the free meal with the purchase of one adult entrée or that the kid's meal is free with a drink. Check with the chains in your area to see which ones offer the kids' meals. There are also a few listings at www.kidseatfree.com.

Go for student services
(for pampering and for food)

Just because you are trying to save money doesn't mean that you can't pamper yourself a little bit. And thank goodness many communities have beauty schools with clinics that are always eager for clients, so that students can get experience. Don't be nervous—believe me, most of these cosmetology and aesthetics programs offer first-class services at a real savings. My experience is that the students who are allowed on the floor with public customers are required to have hundreds of hours of training before they touch you. You can also take comfort in the fact that they are closely supervised as they work on your hair, nails, or face.

There are also massage schools that offer 30-minute to 90-minute massages at about half the going spa massage rates. Most work by appointment, but you can ask about walk-ins, too. One thing you should know is that typically you are expected to tip the students, since that is their only compensation.

One reader of mine put together what she called a "Ms. Cheap Spa Day." She started the day with a Swedish massage at one of the massage schools, then headed to a beauty school for a manicure, pedicure, and facial, and then hit the local mall for a free makeover by one of the makeup salespeople in a department store. Ooh la la!

Speaking of schools, check to see if your city (or one nearby) has a culinary school. If so, the students may operate a restaurant that is open to the public, and you can enjoy a gourmet meal at a budget price. The students may also be able to give you a great price on catering an event! Think what you can save on a wedding or anniversary party while giving these students some super practice. Check with community colleges as well as specialized cooking schools.

– 75 –
Know your benefits at work

I think most people are unaware of *all* the employer benefits that are there for the taking. Most of us know about our insurance, and our sick days and vacation pay, but lots of employers offer other perks that can be helpful. That is why reviewing them every now and then can be a wise move.

My company, Gannett News Service, offers a company-match program for charitable giving where you can give up to $10,000 to the charities of your choice and have the company match your giving.

Locally, our company is linked with a number of partners that offer employees special prices on computers, flowers, office supplies, and other purchases.

My husband works for Vanderbilt University Medical Center, which was recently recognized as one of the 100 best employers in the United States. Vanderbilt not only has lots of perks like opportunities to continue your education, and lots of local partnerships for employee discounts, but a true gem is its college tuition benefit, in which Vanderbilt will pay for 70 percent of the college tuition of employees' children wherever they want to go to college. With us having two daughters, I cannot tell you what an incredible benefit this was for us. But the little perks—like 10 percent off at the dry cleaners or buy-one-get-one-free meals at a restaurant—also help. So don't miss out just because you didn't know.

– 76 –
Put your savings to work

If you save $20 a week clipping coupons, put that amount in your savings account. It may not sound like much at the time, until you calculate you're talking about $10,400 in ten years—and that doesn't include the interest.

~ 77 ~
Learn some new home-improvement skills

You really have no excuse not to tackle home improvement, because the big box stores like The Home Depot and Lowe's offer lots of "how-to" classes for do-it-yourselfers on everything from installing tile and flooring to painting and plumbing and other projects. You can also take advantage of free "how-to" tutorials and other valuable information at the www. lowes.com and www.homedepot.com Web sites as well as sites like www.expertvillage.com and www. diynetwork.com, www.wikihow.com, and www.bejane.com. All of these sites are designed to provide help on home projects—everything from gardening, computer repair, and car repair, to general fix-it projects.

Shop off-season and shop year-round

My M.O. when I enter a store is to head straight for the clearance racks—just to see what they have marked down. Shopping off-season can offer a huge savings—buying swimsuits and sandals and beach towels in the fall and winter, and gloves and scarves and boots and overcoats in the spring and summer.

I mentioned having a gift closet in an earlier entry—and it really does make sense to stock up on all-purpose gifts when you see them at the right price.

The days after each holiday are always good bets. One reader of mine started in January to collect decorations for each holiday as a special wedding gift for a niece who was getting married the next Christmas. She shopped after-holiday sales for Christmas, Valentine's, St. Patrick's Day, Easter, Fourth of July,

Halloween, and Thanksgiving decorations and put together quite an impressive all-holiday package for a pittance.

Another forward-thinking reader did a big chunk of her Christmas shopping the day after Christmas at a sale at Cracker Barrel's gift shop. She went so far as to have the gifts gift wrapped, since Cracker Barrel offered free gift-wrapping at the time. Talk about being ready!

You can also apply this off-season thinking to services like having your firewood delivered and your chimney cleaned in the summer, and having your garden tilled or trees trimmed in the winter, or scheduling a wedding in the least popular seasons.

~ 79 ~
Drink water

I wish I knew how much money I have saved in my adult life by ordering water when I go out to eat, by drinking water instead of soft drinks at the office, and by drinking water with most of my meals at home. And I am talking about ordinary tap water, not the expensive bottled products that seem to have taken over America. I do occasionally buy bottled water for convenience, but believe me, I get a lot of mileage out of my plain old tap water.

– 80 –
Save by sharing

There are so many opportunities to do this by forming informal co-ops to share everything from babysitting, pet sitting, and chores to books, magazines, and coupons. I know of a man who wanted to till a garden and aerate his lawn and figured that several of his neighbors had the same need, so he organized a weekend where the group could rent the equipment together and share it at a fraction of the cost of each one renting it individually.

There is also a group of ladies known as the "weekend warriors" who gather one Saturday a month at a different member's home to work together on a project. They have painted, cooked, cleaned, organized— depending on what the receiving member requested. Not only did they get a formidable project done, they enjoyed their time together.

Babysitting co-ops are very popular with young parents, giving them a chance to get out a little bit in exchange for taking care of a whole group of kids another night. Pet-sitting exchanges work the same way—you keep my pet this weekend, and I keep yours when you take your trip next month.

You can also share the cost of a membership to wholesale clubs like Sam's and Costco. You can share the cost of a wedding gift, or the cost of magazine subscriptions and enjoy more magazines than you can afford alone. It is also smart to share the cost of a trip with friends, saving on gas and accommodations.

Think about what you can sell

People are selling just about everything these days—jewelry (particularly gold), aluminum cans, books, CDs, DVDs and videos, electronics, clothes, furniture, collectibles, maybe even your mother's mink.

There are consignment shops that will sell your furniture and home furnishings and clothes and baby things. There are resale chains with stores like Play it Again Sports for sporting goods, Once Upon a Child for children's items, and Plato's Closet for hip teen and young-adult wear.

Most cities have used–book and music stores that buy, sell, and trade books, music, and movies. There are stores that buy and sell tools, and of course there are lots of seasonal weekend consignment sales that specialize in selling used children's clothes, toys, and equipment. Check this site for sales in your area: www.kidsconsignmentguide.com.

And if you go to your newspaper website, eBay, craigslist, www.etsy.com, or other online auction sites, you can see that people sell everything imaginable—items that have just been sitting around as well as crafty things people are making for sale.

Heck, you can even sell your plasma.

– 82 –
Save every single receipt

I know it's a hassle, but if you ever want to take an item back, these days, you better have the receipt if you want a refund or exchange. I can't blame the retailers for cracking down, but keeping your receipt really is essential if you want to be treated fairly. I have had some readers say they go a step further and attach the tags to the receipt when they save it just to be sure they get their due in an exchange situation. Some stores have what they call an adjustment period where if an item you bought goes on sale within a certain number of days after your purchase, they will give you the difference. And if you are really proactive and find that an item you bought has gone on sale after the adjustment period, you can always return it (with your receipt of course) at the price you paid, and then buy it back at the lower price.

– 83 –
Know your stores

There is nothing wrong with cross shopping, and some stores are definitely better than others for certain things. For example, Walmart has a wonderful price-matching offer in which they will match any competitor's advertised prices. It means you can take your Target flyer, your Walgreen's flyer, and your grocery flyer and get the advertised items at Walmart for the other store's better price. It essentially gives you one-stop shopping at the lowest price, which is a good thing for sure.

But wherever you shop, you need to know the ins and outs of each store and its policies and perks.

You should know when they have their best sales, if their credit card rewards you (and how to make the most of it), if they have customer appreciation opportunities, senior days, kids days, free cookies, free coffee, what their Web site offers, how to get their coupons. I also like to know what they give back to the community and if there are programs that customers can take advantage of where the store gives a percentage of sales to charities in the local community.

I think it is a good idea to know the manager and to take the time to find out about special services, like the butcher trimming your meat, or the seafood station steaming your shrimp, or the deli offering free samples so that you know what you are getting. A good start is simply to go to the customer service counter and ask about special discounts or programs for customers.

Knowing your store is important not only at the grocery store, but at all retail outlets, because I know you'd hate to miss an opportunity for big or small savings.

– 84 –
Get free credit reports

You are entitled to receive one free credit report every 12 months from each of the nationwide consumer credit reporting companies—Equifax, Experian, and TransUnion. This free credit report can be requested through a Web site, by phone, or by mail. The Web site is www.annualCreditReport.com. You can also get information at www.freecreditreport. com.

– 85 –

Stop over-scheduling yourself and the family

Although sports and other extracurricular activities are important, there is a happy medium of scheduled time and family time. If the calendar is too full, consider dropping one or even two activities and creating a free or super-cheap family activity as an alternative. Most of these extra things cost money, so if you cut back, not only do you stop some of the frenzy, but you might stop some of the spending, too.

– 86 –

Find cheap and free entertainment for yourself and the family

This may sound like a challenge, but I think you will be surprised at what all you can find in your community or area that is fun and free—or super cheap—through parks, colleges, libraries, churches, and special days at museums and other attractions. Almost every attraction has a free or half-price day sometime during the year, and it is not that hard to find out when those days are. Most towns have free outdoor concerts in the spring and summer months, and some even offer free classes in the arts for children. Hiking and nature walking can be wonderful for learning and relaxing. Playing tennis costs almost nothing—at least compared to an expensive sport like golf or horseback riding. And keep in mind that just because something costs does not make it any more fun.

– 87 –
Associate with other cheapos

This goes a long way toward keeping you "up" on good deals. With blogs and twitter and old-fashioned phone calls, skinflints can (and should) stick together and share information on sales, good deals, and lucrative offers that pop up every day in all kinds of places.

It is so nice to have a network of shopping buddies so that you can call or e-mail one another when you luck up on triple coupons at a store or special sales on products you know another likes.

It is also nice to have the reinforcement of like-minded people to offer support and encouragement when we want to just say no or when we want to keep things simple and minimalistic.

You can take it a step further and try to win over

non-cheap people to your cheap ways. One of my readers, Wendy Thornton of Nashville, says she suffers from what she calls UCD—"Ultimate Cheapness Disorder"—and one of her tips is to share, share, and share tips, coupons, and other vehicles of cheapness with others.

"If some of the people you hang with are not cheap, help them to become cheap—this can become a learned behavior. Educate them, show them, buy them a coupon book. Use coupons when you go out to eat with them. Make sure they understand that the more you save on fun, the more $$$ you will have to do fun activities. Just let them see, and before you know it, it will become good competition and they will be showing you and telling you about their bargains (and sharing their coupons)."

We are all bombarded with so much media and advertising pushing us to buy, buy, buy. So we all need frugal friends who can help us stick to our guns and say no, no, no. And *no!*

- 88 -

Associate with spendthrifts

This may sound contradictory after that last tip, but it can really pay off if your big-spending friends are fickle and constantly buying new things. We had a neighbor who couldn't settle on a hobby—first he bought a high-end bicycle and then lost interest, then he took up tennis and bought a nice racket and a ball hopper and tons of balls, and then he turned to music and bought a killer keyboard that he played for several months and then became bored with. Of course, there we were waiting in the wings for him to move on to a new pastime, whereupon we would offer to buy his no longer used "toys" for a fraction of what he paid.

Biding your time works with friends who are constantly redecorating, and ones who try different fitness equipment like treadmills or elliptical machines or other newfangled options and then lose interest. Yes, patience is a virtue—and a money-saving one at that.

$-$ 89 $-$
Use store brands

Big savings are possible using store brands, and usually you have nothing to lose since most store brands come with a money-back guarantee for returning the product if you don't like it. You might be surprised to learn that many of the store brands are made right alongside the national brands but just packaged differently. And the store brands are almost universally cheaper because they don't have the expense of national advertising.

To get yourself started, try four or five basic products such as crackers, frozen vegetables, or pasta and see if you can tell the difference. In some cases, the store brands beat out the national ones in taste tests, so check them out.

No matter where you shop, have a list and stick to it

The grocery definitely comes to mind on this one. Not only does having a list keep you organized and save you from making multiple return trips, but if you can stick to it, it saves big money. Supermarket research says that shoppers spend over $2 per minute after they have picked up everything they went to the store to buy. Another telling statistic from the grocery industry is that people who don't shop with a list spend 15 to 20 percent more than those who go with a list. I have no idea how they can figure these stats, but I suspect they are right on. I know that the longer I stay, the more I spend.

I love this fast-shopping tactic that was offered to me by Karen Buckwold of Franklin, Tennessee: "You know how we all go to the grocery and have a list but get distracted especially if we are hungry and end up with a cart full of stuff? Well, I play a little game with myself where I try to see how fast I can be in and out. The checkers must think I'm crazy because I will say, 'I made it in 10 minutes, or whatever. I've saved myself a lot of money.'"

– 91 –

Shop alone and don't shop on an empty stomach

These two tips sound so simple, but they can definitely make a big difference. Shopping with children is not only a distraction, it also adds a big temptation to buy extras that you don't really need—a bag of chips here, a box of cookies there—a carton of chocolate milk . . . and shopping when hungry is definitely trouble for most of us.

~ 92 ~
Know your prices

You won't know something is a bargain unless you know how much the regular price—or a competitor's price—is. Just because a product is displayed prominently in the grocery store with a sign saying "Sale" does not mean it really carries a good price. It is up to you to know the prices of things you buy on a regular basis.

Make your comparisons based on price per ounce or per unit. There can be some big differences. At some stores you may need to consult your calculator, but others post unit prices on the shelf.

— 93 —

Have a menu plan based on what's on sale

If pork chops are on special, it is a good week to plan a meal around pork chops. If you love asparagus, be patient and wait until the price is right and enjoy it all week. Most stores rotate the sale schedule, so there is a good chance you can enjoy a good variety and still buy almost everything at an attractive sale price.

~ 94 ~
Stockpile

Yes, stock up on things you use a lot when the price is right. If you see chicken or ground beef on sale at a great price, buy a lot and immediately go home and freeze it in meal-sized portions that suit your family. You should double-bag everything—using freezer bags that you got at the lowest possible price.

Some of the best non-perishable items to stockpile at the lowest price are canned tomatoes, chicken broth, pasta, tortillas, salsa, and snacks like crackers, raisins, and nuts. Paper towels, toilet paper, and dog food are good prospects, too.

– 95 –
Weigh everything

In the produce department, I weigh everything, not just loose produce. Bags of potatoes, already packaged mushrooms, and heads of lettuce can differ in terms of weight, even though they are all supposed to be the same weight and are selling at the same price. The point is—get the one with the most in it. It's like getting free food. I also compare the salad bar per-pound price for things like cheese, mushrooms, green peppers, and strawberries with other prices in the store. Buying from the salad bar is great if you are making something that you just need a little bit of for a recipe, or if you are cooking up pizzas where you need little bits of different things.

– 96 –
Coupon to the max

In addition to your Sunday newspaper coupons, get extra coupons from relatives, friends, and neighbors, or by buying extra copies of the paper.

More and more deals are offered on grocery sites as well as manufacturers' sites, newspaper sites, and special coupon sites like www.grocerygame.com, a site that charges $10 for eight weeks for you to get information about what's on sale at your grocery and lines them up with coupons that are in your paper. A similar free site is www.couponmom.com, which lists grocery deals by state and has a search tool for coupons. Another site to check is www.e-mealz.com, which takes store sales and plans affordable menus for the week.

Shop stores that double or triple coupons, and try

to be strategic about what coupons you use where—if some double up to 99 cents and some double only to 50 cents, save those larger denominations for the store that will double them.

Combine couponing with sales and other promotions and other tactics: The best of all worlds is when you can find an item on sale—maybe a buy-one-get-one-free deal—and use store coupons and manufacturers' coupons on each item.

And keep your coupons handy—so that you never go to the store without them.

– 97 –

Take advantage of Angel Food Ministries

Take advantage of Angel Food Ministries. If you could get a big box of groceries worth $60 to $70 for $30, wouldn't you do it?

Especially if that $30 price included tax, the only paperwork involved was filling out your order, and your whole shopping expedition took less than five minutes one Saturday morning a month?

It may sound too good to be true, but Angel Food Ministries is there for you, regardless of your income, gender, race, religion, or age. No questions asked.

Nicknamed "blessings in a box" and based in Monroe, Georgia, Angel Food Ministries is a non-denominational organization that works through churches and community organizations in 33 states to provide what they call "grocery relief."

Families and individuals who want to save money on groceries simply sign up, find a host site, see the menu, pay in advance, and then on the distribution day once a month, they pick up their groceries at one of the more than a dozen churches in Middle Tennessee that are host sites for the ministry.

The national Angel Food organization arranges to have the food delivered to the host sites each month where volunteers sort and distribute it. Every month the food selection is different, but participants say you can always count on a good variety and good quality. Generally, one food box is enough to feed a family of four for about a week or a single senior for almost a month.

There are no secondhand items, no damaged or outdated goods, no dented cans or day-old breads. It's all the same quality you would find in the grocery store. Orders and payments are collected by the host sites during the first part of the month, and then pickup is later in the month on a Saturday morning.

See www.angelfoodministries.com for more information about buying food this way, or for information on how you or your church or organization can volunteer or become a host site, call 888-819-3745.

Learn to use the Crock-Pot

Learn to use the Crock-Pot. This nifty cooking contraption has many advantages, not the least of which is coming home from a long day at work to be welcomed by the wonderful smell of a home-cooked dinner like Mom or Grandmama used to slave over the hot stove to make. You can load the pot up in the morning before leaving the house. I sometimes put my food in the night before and put the whole she-bang in the fridge overnight, and then all I have to do in the morning is take it out before work and plug it in).

Other advantages are that the Crock-Pot uses very little energy, it makes cheaper cuts of meat tender and tasty, and the recipes often call for things you already have on hand. Two of my favorite recipes are Crock-

Pot roast and Crock-Pot pork tenderloin. My husband (the real cook at our house) also uses it to make chili and spaghetti, not because it saves money but because it makes it so easy to let a recipe cook all day without having to stir or worry about food sticking or burning down the house.

– 99 –
Read my book

Thanks so much for reading my little book. I truly hope these 99 things will help you with your household budget and have offered you some fresh ways to do more with less in these troubled times. And I hope you will send me your tips for further savings as time goes on. I think we can all help one another with our good ideas. So send your good ideas to me at marymhance@gmail.com. Stay cheap!

Notes